The Infancy Gospel of Thomas

An Intermediate Ancient Greek Reader

C. T. Hadavas

The Infancy Gospel of Thomas

An Intermediate Ancient Greek Reader
Ancient Greek text with vocabulary and commentary

First Edition

© 2014 by C. T. Hadavas

ISBN-13: 978-1494765682
ISBN-10: 1494765683

All images appearing in this edition are in the public domain.

Published by C. T. Hadavas

Cover Design: C. T. Hadavas
Cover Image (front): Virgin Mary with Infant Jesus (contemporary Byzantine-
                          style icon in the author's private collection)

Fonts: (English) Times New Roman; (Greek) Αρισταρχος

hadavasc@beloit.edu

To my undergraduate teachers of Ancient Greek:

Clara Shaw (now Hardy)
Nate Greenberg
Jim Helm
Tom Van Nortwick
Matthew Christ

TABLE OF CONTENTS

INTRODUCTION

The Infancy Gospel of Thomas (IGT) is an excellent text for students who have completed the first year of college-level Ancient Greek or its equivalent. Its length is short, its syntax is generally straightforward, and its narrative is inherently interesting, for it is the only account from the period of early Christianity that tells of the childhood of Jesus.[1]

For those who have studied Attic Greek in their first year, the language and grammar of IGT will for the most part be familiar. All the same, IGT's Greek, known as Koine (ἡ κοινὴ διάλεκτος, *the common language*), does contain several features that will strike the student versed in Attic Greek as different: certain words have taken on new meanings, other words new spellings; grammatical constructions that were either rare or non-existent in earlier Greek have become quite common in this "Later Greek" (denoted throughout this text by the abbreviation LG).[2] The notes and vocabulary lists in this edition point out these differences.

For the student of early Christianity, IGT, along with dozens of other apocryphal texts, serves as a reminder that many different works were

---

[1] It need hardly be said that IGT, despite the claims made by the purported author in the first sentence of the prologue (*I am reporting to you...*), tells a fictional story of the young Jesus' words and deeds.

[2] The phrase "Later Greek" (LG) is one I use to define the various types of Greek that were written and spoken in the centuries following the death of Alexander the Great in 323 BCE up to the early Byzantine period (*c.* 600 CE). For the purposes of this text, Koine Greek, including both the spoken language in all its regional varieties and many, though not all, texts written in the period from 323 BCE up to the the reign of the Roman emperor Constantine the Great (306-337 CE), is synonymous with "Later Greek." Since IGT's text was very likely transmitted both orally and in written form for many centuries after its creation sometime in the mid-2nd century CE, there seem to be a few elements from Late Greek (*c.* 300-600 CE) and, possibly, Medieval Greek (*c.* 600-1453 CE) that are preserved in its textual history. In this edition any non-Classical Greek form or definition is simply identified as LG with the understanding that the vast majority are Koine Greek.

created and employed by various Christian communities that did not make the final "canonical" cut in the fourth century of what texts would be considered authoritative (i.e., biblical) by Church officials. And yet, despite not making it into the Bible, IGT continued to be transmitted, both orally and in written form, throughout the Middle East, Europe, North Africa, Ethiopia, and southwestern Asia for nearly seventeen centuries.[3] In fact, a small part of IGT eventually did become canonical, though in a modified form in a different holy book (see **Appendix 5: IGT 2 and the Qur'an**).

---

[3] IGT's history as a text used by Christians spans the period from *c.* 150 to the early 19th century (the "youngest" manuscript of IGT that exists is a Ukranian one dated 1805). In that time it was translated into more than a dozen languages: Latin, Syriac, Arabic, Ethiopian, Armenian, Georgian, Old Irish, Old Czech, Old French, Middle Bulgarian, Serbian, Croatian, Russian, and Ukranian.

HOW TO USE THIS BOOK

The reader is assumed to have a basic acquaintance with Ancient Greek grammar. All vocabulary found in the passage of IGT on the left page, with the exception of the verb "to be," personal pronouns, and prepositions, is given on the facing page. For most verbs, only the first person singular present active indicative form is given. For verbs with unusual forms (e.g., verbs with deponent futures, second aorists, or with futures and aorists from unrelated stems) the first person singular active forms of the present, future, and aorist are given. For –μι verbs, the second aorist active and, where warranted, the perfect active are also provided. In the Vocabulary entries which list both Classical Greek (CG) and "Later Greek" (LG) definitions, the first category cited is almost certainly the intended meaning in the passage. After a word appears five separate times in the Vocabulary lists it does not appear again (though it will be found, along with all pronouns and prepositions, in the **Glossary** at the end of this book).

At the bottom of the text page are grammatical, syntactical, literary, historical, and cultural notes. In addition, I have on many occasions provided in the notes variant readings from IGT's unusually rich and complex textual history. My guiding principles for selecting such readings were (a) to reveal thematic or theological differences and/or emphases that exist between surviving textual traditions of IGT and (b) to illuminate an interesting textual crux. For a much fuller listing of such variants one can consult Hock's or Burke's editions.[4]

---

[4] R. Hock, *The Infancy Gospels of James and Thomas* (Santa Rosa, CA: Polebridge, 1995), 82-146. Hock's work, which does not include the recently edited – and important – manuscript *Codex Sabaiticus 259*, has, along with all other editions of IGT, recently been superceded by T. Burke's *De infantia Iesu euangelium Thomae graece* (Brepols, 2010), a revised version of his 2001 dissertation. Unlike Hock's edition, however, Burke's will be quite difficult for most individuals to get access to; fortunately, his dissertation is easily accessible online (see **Annotated Bibliography** below).

The phrase "New Testament apocryphal literature" is equivalent to "New Testament non-canonical literature"; i.e., these synonymous phrases simply provide a categorical definition for those texts created by individual Christians or Christian communities from the period of *c.* 50 CE – *c.* 250 CE that did not become part of the New Testament canon.[5] More than fifty of these works – some complete, others surviving only in fragmentary form – are extant, clearly attesting to the vitality and diversity of early Christianity.[6]

While many New Testament apocryphal works provide alternative perspectives on the various theological and socio-cultural issues being discussed and debated within the early Christian communities, others were more focused in seeking to "fill in the blanks" concerning the lives of prominent figures in the religion about whom oral and written traditions offered only limited information. For example, the apocryphal Infancy Gospel of James (*c.* 145 CE) is primarily concerned with the birth and childhood of Mary up until the time she herself gives birth to Jesus. Mary is a shadowy figure in the gospel of Mark, and even in the three later gospels where her role has increased, little is actually said about her. The Infancy Gospel of James, however, seems to have been created to satisfy the desire of early Christians for stories about who Mary was as a child, illustrating for believers the special nature she possessed that qualified her to be the mother of God's son. Indeed, the Infancy Gospel of James is the first text that asserts Mary's perpetual virginity before, during and after the birth of Jesus, an idea that continues to be held about her in the Catholic and Eastern Orthodox Churches today.

---

[5] A few apocryphal texts may be from the 1st century or contain elements from that century (e.g., the Gospel of Thomas); the majority seem to have been created in the 2nd century (e.g., IGT), with a handful being dated to the first half of the 3rd century (e.g., the Acts of Peter and Andrew).

[6] New Testament apocrypha include works of the apostolic fathers, Jewish-Christian gospels, infancy gospels, gnostic gospels, sayings gospels, epistles, apocalypses, and early missionary stories.

Jesus (*c.* 4 BC – *c.* 30 CE) is the central figure of the New Testament gospels and plays a prominent, albeit indirect, role in other New Testament texts. Despite this seemingly extensive coverage, what is actually narrated about his life and person in these works is chronologically quite limited. In fact, the earliest Christian writings about him, Paul's letters (*c.* 51-58 CE), focus principally on the post-resurrection Christ, since Paul never knew (nor valued to any great extent) the person, teaching and deeds of the historical Jesus. The first "biographer" of Jesus, Mark, begins his gospel (*c.* 70 CE) with the adult Jesus, and tells his audience nothing about what happened in the first three decades of his subject's life. Matthew (*c.* 75-100 CE) and Luke (*c.* 75-100 CE), both of whom used Mark as a source for their gospels, do narrate the birth of Jesus (though their accounts differ somewhat), but then either provide no further information on him until he becomes an adult (Matthew) or only describe one short incident when he is twelve years old: Jesus' staying behind in Jerusalem after Passover where he is disovered by his parents conversing with the scholars in the Temple (Luke 2:41-52).[7]

IGT, then, seems to have been written in order to extend a Christian's knowledge of Jesus chronologically by providing information on his childhood years. Although its narrative can function as an independent work, IGT also seems to have been crafted to supplement Luke's very limited account of Jesus' childhood, slotting in between Luke 2:40 (Jesus as an infant) and 2:41 (Jesus as a twelve-year old in the Temple discussing the Hebrew Scriptures with the scholars). IGT even replays the narrative of Luke 2:41-52 as its conclusion (though with some interesting modifications), signaling, in effect, that the reader can now turn to Luke for the rest of the story.[8]

---

[7] John's gospel, which stands apart from the other three gospel accounts (partly because it does not seem to make much, if any, use of Mark's gospel as a source), says nothing about the earthly birth or childhood of Jesus, and, like Mark, begins its narrative with Jesus as an adult.

[8] For a thematic and stylistic comparison of this section of Luke's gospel to the ending of IGT, see **Appendix 1: Luke 2:41-52 and IGT 19**.

But despite its narrative connection to Luke's gospel, IGT's view of Jesus, even as a child, may be closer in certain ways to the figure of Jesus as found in John's gospel (*c.* 90-100 CE).[9] So IGT is not simply a text that answers the question: "What did Jesus do as a child (that Luke do not mention)?" It also attempts to answer such questions as: "What kind of individual was Jesus as a child? Did he act like most young boys, though with the added benefit/burden of supernatural powers? Can one see in his behavior and deeds aspects of the adult Jesus who appears in the gospels of Mark, Matthew, or Luke? And did Jesus, even as a child, share certain characteristics with the more "other-worldly" figure of John's gospel?"

---

[9] R. Aasgaard, *The Childhood of Jesus: Decoding the Apocryphal Infancy Gospel of Thomas* (Eugene: Cascade Books, 2009), 120-121, provides a list of allusions in IGT to various biblical texts, the majority being from John's gospel, after which he infers that the theological similarities between the two are "so marked that this too supports IGT's knowledge of John." Later, when exploring the theological and Christological aspects of IGT, Aasgaard concludes (156) that "IGT's divine Jesus owes particularly much to the gospel of John."

The Language

IGT is written in Koine Greek, the most common spoken and written form of Greek in use from the death of Alexander the Great (323 BCE) to the reign of the Roman emperor Constantine the Great (306-337 CE). The literary range of Koine Greek texts is quite large, and includes writers as diverse in style as Plutarch (*c*. 46 – *c*. 120 CE) and the unknown author of the Gospel of Mark (*c*. 70 CE), both of whom were biographers and contemporaries. IGT's narrative, most likely composed in some form in the 2nd century CE, is in certain respects similar to the language found in Mark's gospel, John's gospel, and Revelation. Like those works, IGT possesses thematic, syntactical, and grammatical features that suggest a certain degree of oral composition.[10]

Although there are many (mostly small) differences between Classical Greek and Koine Greek, perhaps the most important for the beginning-intermediate student are those that involve vocabulary and spelling.[11] With respect to the former, the number of loanwords from other languages increased (in IGT, e.g., ὁ κράββατος, *bed*, *cot*, is probably from Macedonian; τὸ παλ(λ)ίον, *cloak*, from Latin). In addition, CG words sometimes simply expanded their semantic domains for cultural or religious reasons (e.g., τὸ ἔθνος, when used by a Christian or Jewish author means *Gentile* [i.e., non-Jew], while in CG and in non-Christian/Jewish LG authors it means *tribe* or *nation*; LG extends CG's biological meaning of ὁ ἀδελφός, *brother*, to include a member of a religious community).

---

[10] For a list of the oral aspects of IGT's narrative and how these impact one's understanding of the text and its reconstruction, see Aasgaard, *The Childhood of Jesus*, 25-34.

[11] Other differences include: (1) the rarity, then eventual disappearance of the optative mood (there are no optatives in IGT); (2) the decrease in the use of particles (there is only one particle in IGT, δή) and conjunctions; (3) the increase in the use of prepositions (often with new meanings) and the consequent decrease of the dative case without prepositions to express meaning (even its "core" function of denoting the indirect object is being slowly encroached upon by πρός + acc.; cf., e.g., IGT 3:2); (4) the preference for direct discourse over indirect discourse; (5) the middle voice is often replaced with the active voice + reflexive pronouns.

With respect to spelling, Koine Greek will sometimes use forms identical to those of non-Attic Greek dialects (e.g., Ionic's γίνομαι is used in place of Attic prose's γίγνομαι). In addition, phonetic similarities occasionally led to confusion in the spelling of indicative and subjunctive verb forms (e.g., at IGT 12:1 σπείρει = σπείρη).

In IGT one also notices the Koine Greek fondness for:

1. Periphrastic constructions in place of indicative verb forms.

IGT often employs the periphrastic construction of present or perfect participle + the imperfect of the verb εἰμί in place of CG's preference for the imperfect tense (e.g., IGT 2:1 has παίζων ἦν instead of ἔπαιζε).

2. Diminutives.

In Koine Greek the diminutive often loses any special meaning it may have conveyed in CG (i.e., of size, of affection, or its use as a pejorative) and simply takes the place of the original word. For example, in Koine Greek the word for "ear" is most often τὸ ὠτίον (cf. IGT 5:4), the diminutive form (i.e., *little ear*) of the CG word for "ear," τὸ οὖς. Occasionally in Koine Greek the diminutive may coexist with its non-diminutive predecessor. For example, in IGT both τὸ παιδίον and ὁ παῖς are found; in certain cases τὸ παιδίον may denote a younger age than the more temporally wide-ranging ὁ παῖς.

3. καί.

καί is used more frequently in Koine Greek texts, sometimes to the point of redundancy (e.g., in IGT 9:1, 11:2, 17:2, 17:4). Other Koine texts that share IGT's fondness for καί include the gospels of Mark and John and the final book of the Bible, Revelation. Such extensive use of καί seems to be evidence of oral composition, at least at some stage in the history of these works.[12]

---

[12] This frequent use of καί was thought by previous generations of scholars to be a possible indicator of a Semitic substrate and/or provide evidence for the influence of Semitic syntax on certain Koine texts. Such possibilities, however, are considered less likely by contemporary scholars.

4. Parataxis.

Connected to IGT's fondness for καί is its frequent use of parataxis (independent clauses joined by coordinating connectives such as καί and δέ); correlatively, IGT's use of hypotaxis (the use of dependent clauses) is far less common than in CG.

The text used in this book is to a great extent derived from Hock's edition, which in turn is based on Tischendorf A. Although there are numerous instances where Hock deviates from Tischendorf A, the most significant is in Chapter 6, where he follows the longer text for this chapter found in *Codex Atheniensis 355*. My text deviates on occasion from Hock's (most notably by including readings from *Codex Sabiticus 259*, which was not available to Hock), makes minor corrections to his text, and employs formatting that is designed to better serve beginning-intermediate students (e.g., all direct discourse is marked by the use of quotation marks).

Recently, Aasgaard has pointed out that Hock's edition, like Tischendorf's before it, is "problematic."[13] Indeed, given the likely hybrid oral-literary nature of IGT's development, Hock's version cannot be an approximation of the so-called original second-century text (called the "autograph"). Hock himself has recognized this, and states that this is not really the purpose of his edition.[14] What Hock's text, with its conflation of the various families of the Greek text along with a smattering of other versional accounts, captures – at least to some degree – is the rich diversity of IGT's textual history.[15]

---

[13] Aasgaard, *The Childhood of Jesus*, 8.

[14] Hock, *The Infancy Gospels of James and Thomas*, 101.

[15] Much work has been done in the past two decades on more accurately identifying IGT's various textual traditions/families (called by scholars "rescensions," though Aasgaard, *The Childhood of Jesus*, 31-3, dislikes the term when applied to IGT's manuscript history since it privileges the ideal of a single "ur" text from which all others are descended). The individual who has done the most significant and important work in this field is Tony Chartrand-Burke (more recently just Burke), whose research may eventually prove decisive in convincing a majority of scholars who work on early Christian texts that a somewhat shorter narrative version of IGT than that of Tischendorf A, such as the one in *Codex Sabaiticus 259*, is closer to the now lost second-century text. Despite Burke's contributions, however, the distinct possibility exists of a lengthy oral-literary interdependent period (posited by Gero, Hock, and Aasgaard). This suggests that the hypothetical early text (reflected to some degree by *Codex Sabaiticus 259*) would only be one strand of many – possibly, but not necessarily, more important than others – that contributed to the diverse textual history of IGT.

The two manuscript families for the Greek text cited in the notes in this student edition follow those established by the 19th-century German scholar Constantin von Tischendorf. These are:

Tischendorf A: based on four manuscripts from the 15th-16th centuries, this text by Tischendorf (2nd ed. 1876) contains the longer, 19-chapter version of IGT.

Tischendorf B: based on a single manuscript from the 14th-15th century (*Codex Sinaiticus Gr453*), this text by Tischendorf (2nd ed. 1876) contains a shorter, 11-chapter version of IGT that often differs considerably from Tischendorf A, especially in its extensive abridgments of the sayings and dialogue episodes.

In addition, I have also included in the notes two important manuscripts that have been discovered since Tischendorf's editions appeared in 1876:

CA 355 (= *Codex Atheniensis 355*): called Greek C by Hock, this late 15th-century manuscript contains, in addition to other differences with Tischendorf A and Tischendorf B, a longer and rather distinctive version of Chapter 6.

CS 259 (= *Codex Sabaiticus 259*): although the existence of this manuscript (dated 1089-90, making it the earliest surviving Greek version of IGT) was known to Hock, it had not yet been published in 1995 and so was not employed by him in his edition. Its text is shorter than Tischendorf A, both in many of the individual narratives and in the fact that it lacks Tischendorf A's chs. 17 and 18. And despite the fact that it exhibits some elements that can be considered later than Tischendorf A, it has come to be seen by Burke and Aasgaard – probably correctly – as representative of a form of IGT in Greek earlier than that of any other family.[16]

---

[16] *Codex Sabaiticus 259*'s importance was first noted by S. Voicu, "Notes sur l'histoire du texte de L'Histoire de L'Enfance de Jesus," in *La Fable Apocryphe*, 2 vols., ed. by P. Geoltrain *et al.*, 2.119-32. (Tournhout: Brepols, 1989-1991), 120.

Lastly, one will see in the notes the following designation:

Greek-Slav: a controversial "reconstructed text" that was translated back into Greek from the Slavonic versions by A. de Santos Otero in 1967.[17] It seems clear that the Slavonic translations were made from a now-lost Greek original of the 10th or 11th century,[18] so the use of these texts to assist one in understanding the Greek textual tradition of IGT is not without some merits.

Differences from Hock's text:

This text	Hock's text
6.11 ἐφιμώθησαν (CS 259)	ἐθυμώθησαν (CA 355)
6:15 αὐτόν. (CS 259)	αὐτὸν ἕως ὥρας πολλάς. (CA 355)
6:23 καὶ πρόσχες πῶς ὧδε ἔχει (CS 259)	ὧδέ πως ἔχει· (CA 355)
13:2 τοῦ σοῦ μέρους (CS 259)	τοῦ μέσου μέρους (Tischendorf A)
17:4 ἐστιν (*Codex hist. Gr 91*)	ἦν (Tischendorf A)

---

[17] A. de Santos Otero, *Das Kirchenslavische Evangelium des Thomas* (PTS 6; Berlin: Walter de Gruyter, 1967). For a summary of the scholarly reception of Santos Otero's translation together with further references, see T. Rosén, *The Slavonic Translation of the Apocryphal Infancy Gospel of Thomas* (Acta Universitatis Upsaliensis. *Studia Slavica Upsaliensia*, 39; Uppsala: 1997), 22-25.

[18] Rosén, *The Slavonic Translation*, 166.

Good succinct introductions to IGT are provided by H-J. Klauck's "The Infancy Gospel of Thomas," in *Apocryphal Gospels: An Introduction*, translated by Brian McNeil (London: T&T Clark, 2003), 73-81 and T. Chartrand-Burke's "The *Infancy Gospel of Thomas*," in *The Non-Canonical Gospels*, edited by P. Foster (London: T&T Clark, 2008), 126-138.

A slightly more detailed introduction, along with helpful notes to various parts of the text, can be found in R. Hock's *The Infancy Gospels of James and Thomas* (Santa Rosa, CA: Polebridge, 1995), 82-146.

The most important research on IGT from the previous generation is S. Gero's "The Infancy Gospel of Thomas: A Study of the Textual and Literary Problems," *Novum Testamentum* 13 (1971), 46-80. Gero employed form-critical analysis of IGT's individual episodes[19] and argued strongly in favor of their oral transmission throughout much of IGT's history as a narrative work.

The best recent work on IGT is R. Aasgaard's *The Childhood of Jesus: Decoding the Apocryphal Infancy Gospel of Thomas* (Eugene: Cascade Books, 2009), which covers nearly every conceivable topic on this short but enigmatic text. Although many of Aasgaard's ideas will not convince everyone, his text has laid out the most important (and interrelated) questions scholars should be asking with regard to future work on IGT.[20] Of particular value is his inclusion of the Greek text of *Codex Sabaiticus 259* with an English translation, thus making this critical witness to the textual tradition of IGT easily available to students and scholars.

---

[19] Form criticism is a method of textual analysis, applied especially to the Bible, in which the origin and history of certain passages are traced by isolating their literary forms (as, e.g., miracle story, saying, apothegm, etc.), on the assumption that they were fixed by oral tradition prior to being written down.

[20] Reviews of Aasgaard's work include T. Burke, *Journal of Early Christian Studies*, Volume 18, Number 3 (Fall 2010), 470-471 and E. Norelli, *Bryn Mawr Classical Review* (in French): http://bmcr.brynmawr.edu/2010/2010-08-09.html

Much of Aasgaard's work derives from important research on the textual tradition of IGT done by Chartrand-Burke in his 2001 dissertation, "The Infancy Gospel of Thomas: The Text, its Origins, and its Transmission," which is available online (as of March 2014):

http://www.collectionscanada.gc.ca/obj/s4/f2/dsk3/ftp05/NQ63782.pdf

Although the majority of Chartrand-Burke's dissertation is devoted to the textual tradition of IGT, its third section covers such topics as the Christology of IGT and the way children were viewed in Roman antiquity.

Chartrand-Burke's dissertation has been revised and published in Brepol's series *Corpus Christianorum Series Apocryphorum* (CCSA 17) as *De infantia Iesu euangelium Thomae graece*, ed. T. Burke (Brepols: 2010). This work contains the main representatives of what Burke has identified as the four principal rescensions of the Greek text, and has completely superceded all previous research on IGT's long and complex textual history.[21]

---

[21] Unfortunately, Burke's edition will probably be inaccessible to the vast majority of individuals and institutions on account of its prohibitive cost (currently $648.00 in the U.S.).

ENGLISH TRANSLATIONS

Burke, T. *The Childhood of the Saviour (Infancy Gospel of Thomas): A New Translation*, 2009. http://www.tonyburke.ca/infancy-gospel-of-thomas/the-childhood-of-the-saviour-infancy-gospel-of-thomas-a-new-translation/

Cullmann, O. "The Infancy Gospel of Thomas." In *New Testament Apocrypha*, edited by W. Schneemelcher; rev. ed. trans. R. McL. Wilson. Louisville: Westminster/John Knox, 1991, 1.439-52.

Ehrman, B. and Z. Pleše. *The Apocryphal Gospels: Texts and Translations*. New York: Oxford University Press, 2011, 2-23.

Elliott, J. K. *The Apocryphal New Testament*. Oxford: Clarendon, 1993, 68-83.

Hock, R. *The Infancy Gospels of James and Thomas*. Santa Rosa, CA: Polebridge, 1995, 83-143.

James, M. R. *The Apocryphal New Testament being the Apocryphal Gospels, Acts, Epistles, and Apocalypses*. Oxford: Clarendon, 1924, 49-65.

ELECTRONIC RESOURCES

Two websites offer much comparative material for students who want to explore IGT in its various forms:

http://www.tonyburke.ca/infancy-gospel-of-thomas/

Maintained by Tony Burke, this website "is," as he states, "dedicated largely to providing up-to-date English translations of the available witnesses to the text. Most readers of IGT are familiar with the longer 19-chapter form made popular by Constantin von Tischendorf in 1856. There has been much progress over the intervening decades since Tischendorf's edition. The texts presented here represent the latest advances in the effort to sort through the evidence."

Burke's site is most useful for providing four things:

1. English translations of the following versional languages IGT: Syriac, Ethiopic, Old Latin, Georgian, Irish, Slavonic, Late Latin, and Arabic.
2. A translation of Burke's reconstruction of what he believes the 2nd-century text of IGT might have looked like.
3. A link to his 2001 dissertation on IGT in PDF form.
4. A link to the section on IGT at Peter Kirby's site on early Christian writings:

http://www.earlychristianwritings.com/infancythomas.html

Kirby's site contains several (mostly older) translations from the various recensions established by Tischendorf, thus providing easy (though it must be noted somewhat outdated and incomplete) access to the different forms of IGT's Greek text.

ABBREVIATIONS

acc.(usative)
act.(ive voice)
adj.(ective)
adv.(erb)
aor.(ist)
c. circa
cf. compare (Latin *confer*)
CG = Classical Greek (i.e., Greek in use in the 5th and 4th centuries BCE)
ch.(apter)
comp.(arative)
dat.(ive)
dep.(opent)
fem.(inine)
fut.(ure)
gen.(itive)
gen.(itive) abs.(olute)
IGT = Infancy Gospel of Thomas
impera.(tive)
imperf.(ect)
indecl.(inable)
indic.(ative)
inf.(initive)
LG = Later Greek (i.e., Greek in use from the Hellenistic to the early
    Byzantine period, i.e., 323 BCE – *c*. 600 CE)
masc.(uline)
mid.(dle voice)
neut.(er)
n.(ote)
nom.(inative)
NT = New Testament
p./pp. page(s)
part.(iciple)
pass.(ive voice)
perf.(ect)
pl.(ural)
pluperf.(ect)
pres.(ent)
rel.(ative) pron.(oun)
sc. = supply or understand
sing.(ular)
subj.(ect)
subju.(nctive)
superl.(ative)
Synoptic = the Gospels of Mark, Matthew, and Luke
voc.(ative)

Παιδικὰ τοῦ κυρίου ἡμῶν Ἰησοῦ Χριστοῦ

The Childhood Deeds of our Lord Jesus Christ

Παιδικὰ τοῦ κυρίου ἡμῶν Ἰησοῦ Χριστοῦ

PROLOGUE

1. ἀναγγέλλω ὑμῖν ἐγὼ Θωμᾶς Ἰσραηλίτης πᾶσι τοῖς ἐξ

ἐθνῶν ἀδελφοῖς γνωρίσαι τὰ παιδικὰ καὶ μεγαλεῖα τοῦ

κυρίου ἡμῶν Ἰησοῦ Χριστοῦ, ὅσα ἐποίησεν γεννηθεὶς ἐν

τῇ χώρᾳ ἡμῶν. οὗ ἡ ἀρχὴ οὕτως.

××

Ἰησοῦ: Ἰησοῦς is the Greek rendition of the Hebrew name Yeshua.
Χριστοῦ: *of the Anointed One/Messiah*; later a proper name (i.e., *Christ*).
The Greek word is a translation of the Hebrew *Mašîaḥ* ("Messiah"), which
means "(the One) Anointed with Holy Oil." In Jewish eschatology, the term
Messiah refers to a future Jewish leader from the Davidic line who will be
anointed with holy oil (i.e., "crowned king") and who will then be the ruler of
God's kingdom. Jesus came to be called "Jesus Christ" (i.e., "Jesus, the
Anointed One/Messiah") by his followers after his death and believed
resurrection.

1:1 ἀναγγέλλω ὑμῖν: the only canonical gospel that begins with a first-
person address to its reader(s) is that of Luke; so perhaps it is no surprise that
IGT is specifically designed to supplement Luke's account of Jesus' childhood,
slotting in between Luke 2:40 (Jesus as an infant) and 2:41 (Jesus as a twelve-
year old in the Temple discussing the Hebrew Scriptures with the scholars).
ἀναγγέλλω and ὑμῖν have appostional elaboration in an interlocking A B A¹ B¹
sequence: ἐγὼ Θωμᾶς Ἰσραηλίτης and πᾶσι τοῖς ἐξ ἐθνῶν ἀδελφοῖς.
Θωμᾶς: *Thomas*, an Aramaic word that means "twin"; in origin it is not
a given name but an epithet of a New Testament figure, Judas Thomas, the
second Judas of the Apostles (hence his appellation "twin" to distinguish him
from his more infamous namesake, Judas Iscariot). Thomas appears throughout
John's gospel (11:16, 14:5, 21:2), but is most famous for the episode in which
he expresses strong doubt in the resurrection of Jesus (20:24-28). Hock (105)
notes that in apocryphal literature he has an even larger role (see, e.g., the
Gospel of Thomas and the Acts of Thomas). γνωρίσαι: inf. of purpose
(rare in CG prose). γεννηθεὶς: masc. nom. sing. aor. pass. part. < γεννάω.
ἐν τῇ χώρᾳ ἡμῶν: i.e., the ancient Roman province of Judea (modern-day
Israel/Palestine). οὗ ἡ ἀρχὴ οὕτως = ἡ ἀρχὴ οὗ ἐστιν οὕτως.

Vocabulary

ἀδελφός, ὁ, brother

ἀναγγέλλω, bring back tidings of, report

ἀρχή, ἡ, beginning

γεννάω, be father of, give birth to; (pass.) be born

γνωρίζω, make known

ἔθνος, ἔθνους, τό, (LG) Gentile (i.e., non-Jew); (CG) tribe, people

Θωμᾶς, ὁ, Thomas

Ἰησοῦς, Ἰησοῦ, Ἰησοῦ, Ἰησοῦν, ὁ, Jesus

Ἰσραηλίτης, -ου, ὁ, Israelite

κύριος, ὁ, (LG) Lord (title of God in the Old Testament and of Jesus Christ in the New Testament); (CG) lord, master, head (of a family/household); sir

μεγαλεῖος, -α, -ον, magnificent, splendid, mighty

ὅσος, -η, -ον, as great as, as much as; (pl.) as many as

ὅς, ἥ, ὅ, rel. pron., who, whose, whom, which, that

οὕτως, adv., so, thus; as follows

παιδικός, -ή, -όν, child-like, playful, pertaining to one's childhood; in CG τὰ παιδικά is a term of romantic affection meaning darling or favorite

πᾶς, πᾶσα, πᾶν, all, every, whole

ποιέω, make, produce, create; do

Χριστός, ὁ, the Anointed One/Messiah; later a proper name (i.e., Christ)

χώρα, ἡ, land

An Alternative Beginning

The beginning of the oldest surviving Greek manuscript of IGT, the 11th-century *Codex Sabaiticus 259*, is as follows (f. 66r-v):

τά παιδικὰ μεγαλεῖα τοῦ δεσπότου ἡμῶν καὶ
σωτῆρος Ἰησοῦ Χριστοῦ

1. ἀναγκαῖον ἡγησάμην ἐγὼ Θωμᾶς Ἰσραηλίτης γνωρίσαι πᾶσιν τοῖς ἐξ ἐθνῶν ἀδελφοῖς ὅσα ἐποίησεν ὁ κύριος ἡμῶν Ἰησοῦς ὁ Χριστὸς γεννηθεὶς ἐν τῇ χώρᾳ ἡμῶν Βηθλεὲμ κώμῃ Ναζαρέτ. ὧν ἡ ἀρχή ἐστιν αὕτη.

The Mighty Childhood Deeds of our Master and Savior Jesus Christ

1. *I, Thomas the Israelite, have considered it necessary to make known to all the brothers of the Gentiles the things that our Lord Jesus Christ did after he had been born in our land of Bethlehem in the village of Nazareth. The beginning of which is this:*

---

2. τοῦτο τὸ παιδίον Ἰησοῦς πενταέτης γενόμενος παίζων ἦν

ἐν διαβάσει ῥύακος, ² καὶ τὰ ῥέοντα ὕδατα συνήγαγεν εἰς

λάκκους, καὶ ἐποίει αὐτὰ εὐθέως καθαρά, καὶ λόγῳ μόνῳ

ἐπέταξεν αὐτά. ³ καὶ ποιήσας πηλὸν τρυφερὸν ἔπλασεν

ἐξ αὐτοῦ στρουθία δώδεκα· καὶ ἦν σάββατον ὅτε ταῦτα

ἐποίησεν. ἦσαν δὲ καὶ ἄλλα παιδία πολλὰ παίζοντα σὺν

αὐτῷ.

✕✕

2:1 παίζων ἦν: LG often employs the periphrastic construction of pres. part. +
the imperf. of the verb εἰμί in place of CG's preference for the imperf. tense
(cf. also ἦσαν, παίζοντα in the last sentence of this section). CS 259 simply
has ἔπαιζεν.

2:2 ἐποίει...ἐπέταξεν αὐτά: the young Jesus' control over nature appears
also at 7:4. In the Synoptic account, Jesus' powers over nature appear only
in his calming of the storm (Mark 4:35-41; Matt. 8:23-27; Luke 8:22-25).

2:3 στρουθία: a diminutive form of στρουθός; in LG, however, the diminutive
often loses any special meaning it may have conveyed in CG (i.e., of size, of
affection, or its use as a pejorative) and simply takes the place of the original
word. Occasionally the diminutive in LG may coexist with its non-diminutive
predecessor (e.g., in this section, παιδίον and παῖς, where παιδίον may
sometimes denote a younger age than the more temporally wide-ranging παῖς).
δώδεκα: perhaps an allusion to the twelve forefathers/tribes of Israel or
(more likely) to the twelve apostles. σάββατον: in the Hebrew tradition,
this is a weekly day of rest, observed from sundown on Friday until the
appearance of three stars in the sky on Saturday night. Technically, "playing"
on the Sabbath is not officially proscribed, but the general consensus is that any
activity on the Sabbath that is creative, or that exercises control or dominion
over one's environment is prohibited.

4

Vocabulary

αὐτός, -ή, -ό, (CG, pron. in gen., dat., acc.) *him, her, it, them*; (LG, pron. in all cases) *he, she, it, they*

διάβασις, -εως, ἡ, *ford*

δώδεκα, *twelve*

γί(γ)νομαι, *become*

ἐπιτάσσω, *order, command*

εὐθέως, adv., *immediately, at once*

καθαρός, -ά, -όν, *clean, pure*

λάκκος, ὁ, *pond*

λόγος, ὁ, *word, speech*

μονός, -ή, -όν, *alone, only, single*

οὗτος, αὕτη, τοῦτο, *this*; (pl.) *these*

ὅτε, adv., *when*

παιδίον, τό, (diminutive of παῖς, ὁ or ἡ) *little* or *young child, child*

παίζω, *play*

πενταετής, -ές, *five years old*

πηλός, ὁ, *clay, earth, mud*

πλάσσω, *form, mold, shape*

ποιέω, *make, produce, create; do*

πολύς, πολλή, πολύ, *much*; (pl.) *many*

ῥέω, *flow, run*

ῥύαξ, -ακος, ὁ, *rushing stream*

σάββατον, τό, *Sabbath*

στρουθίον, τό, (LG diminutive of στρουθός, ὁ or ἡ) *sparrow*

συνάγω, συνάξω, συνήγαγον, *bring* or *gather together*

τρυφερός, -ά, -όν, *soft*; in CL the adj. normally means *delicate, dainty*

ὕδωρ, ὕδατος, τό, *water*

⁴ ἰδὼν δέ τις Ἰουδαῖος ἃ ἐποίει ὁ Ἰησοῦς ἐν σαββάτῳ

παίζων ἀπῆλθε παραχρῆμα καὶ ἀνήγγειλε τῷ πατρὶ αὐτοῦ

Ἰωσήφ· "ἰδοὺ τὸ παιδίον σού ἐστιν ἐπὶ τὸ ῥυάκιον, καὶ

λαβὼν πηλὸν ἔπλασεν πουλία δώδεκα, καὶ ἐβεβήλωσεν τὸ

σάββατον."

⁵ καὶ ἐλθὼν Ἰωσὴφ ἐπὶ τὸν τόπον καὶ ἰδὼν ἀνέκραξεν

αὐτῷ λέγων· "διὰ τί ταῦτα ποιεῖς ἐν σαββάτῳ ἃ οὐκ ἔξεστι

ποιεῖν;"

⁶ ὁ δὲ Ἰησοῦς συγκροτήσας τὰς χεῖρας αὐτοῦ ἀνέκραξε

τοῖς στρουθίοις καὶ εἶπεν αὐτοῖς· "ὑπάγετε, πετάσατε καὶ

μιμνήσκεσθέ μου οἱ ζῶντες." καὶ πετασθέντα τὰ στρουθία

ὑπῆγον κράζοντα.

✕✕

2:4 παίζων: *while playing*; an adverbial/circumstantial use of the part. with
temporal force. **αὐτοῦ** = (CG) ἑαυτοῦ. **ἐβεβήλωσεν τὸ σάββατον**:
cf. Matthew 12:5, where Jesus replies to the Pharisees, who have accused his
disciples of acting unlawfully on the Sabbath because they plucked grain in a
field and ate it, that David acted unlawfully on the Sabbath in a time of need by
taking bread from the Temple, and that the actions of the priests of the Temple
τὸ σάββατον βεβηλοῦσιν (*violate the Sabbath*), and yet they are innocent. In
the NT Jesus is often charged by religious authorities for violating the Sabbath
(see, e.g., Mark 2:23-3, 3:1-6; Luke 13:10-17, 14:2-6; John 5:2-16, 9:1-17).
2:5 διὰ τί: literally, *on account of what thing*, i.e., *why*.
2:6 πετάσατε: though πέτομαι is a dep. verb, in LG the aor. indic. and imper.
forms are often act. in meaning. **οἱ ζῶντες**: an appostional subject phrase,
as if modifying (an understood) στρουθοί instead of στρουθία. CS 259 lacks
μιμνήσκεσθέ μου and has ὡς ζῶντες (*like living* [sc. sparrows]) for οἱ
ζῶντες.

6

Vocabulary

ἀναγγέλλω, *bring back tidings of, report*

ἀνακράζω, *cry out*

ἀπέρχομαι, ἀπελεύσομαι, ἀπῆλθον, *go, go away, depart*

βεβηλόω, (LG) *desecrate, violate*

δώδεκα, *twelve*

ἔξεστι(ν), (impersonal + inf.) *it is allowed* or *possible*

ἔρχομαι, ἐλεύσομαι, ἦλθον, *come, go*

ζάω, (unattested hypothetical form) *live, be alive*

ἰδού, adv., *look!*

Ἰουδαῖος, ὁ, *Judean, Jew*

Ἰωσήφ, ὁ, (indecl.), *Joseph*

κράζω, *cry out, shriek*

λαμβάνω, λήψομαι, ἔλαβον, *take*

λέγω, ἐρῶ, εἶπον, *say, speak, tell*

μιμνήσκω, *remind*; (mid./pass.) *remember*

ὁράω, ὄψομαι, εἶδον, *see*

παιδίον, τό, (diminutive of παῖς, ὁ or ἡ) *little* or *young child, child*

παίζω, *play*

πατήρ, πατρός, ὁ, *father*

πέτομαι, *fly*

πηλός, ὁ, *clay, earth, mud*

πλάσσω, *form, mold, shape*

ποιέω, *make, produce, create; do*

πουλίον, τό, (LG, sometimes spelled πουλλίον) *bird*

ῥυάκιον, τό, (diminutive of ῥύαξ, -ακος, ὁ) *(small) rushing stream*

σάββατον, τό, *Sabbath*

στρουθίον, τό, (LG diminutive of στρουθός, ὁ or ἡ) *sparrow*

συγκροτέω, *strike together*; (with χεῖρας) *clap one's hands (in joy)*

τόπος, ὁ, *place*

ὑπάγω, ὑπάξω, ὑπήγαγον, (LG) *go, go away, depart*

χείρ, χειρός, ἡ, *hand*

⁷ Ἰδόντες δὲ οἱ Ἰουδαῖοι ἐθαμβήθησαν, καὶ ἀπελθόντες

διηγήσαντο τοῖς πρώτοις αὐτῶν ὅπερ εἶδον πεποιηκότα τὸν

Ἰησοῦν.

3. ὁ δὲ υἱὸς Ἄννα τοῦ γραμματέως ἦν ἑστὼς ἐκεῖ μετὰ τοῦ

Ἰησοῦ, καὶ λαβὼν κλάδον ἰτέας ἐξέχεε τὰ ὕδατα ἃ συνήγαγεν

ὁ Ἰησοῦς. ² ἰδὼν δὲ ὁ Ἰησοῦς τὸ γινόμενον ἠγανάκτησε, καὶ

εἶπε πρὸς αὐτόν· "Σοδομίτα, ἄσεβες καὶ ἀνόητε, τί ἠδίκησάν

σε οἱ λάκκοι καὶ τὰ ὕδατα; ἰδοὺ νῦν καὶ σὺ ὡς δένδρον

ἀποξηρανθῇς, οὐ μὴ ἐνέγκῃς φύλλα οὔτε ῥίζαν οὔτε καρπόν."

✕✕

2:7 τοῖς πρώτοις: sc. ἀνθρώποις; i.e., the leaders of the village.
πεποιηκότα: masc. acc. sing. perf. act. part. < ποιέω.

3:1 Ἄννα: gen.; in the NT it is the name of the high priest (see Luke 3:2; John
18:13, 24; Acts 4:6). τοῦ γραμματέως: in apposition to Ἄννα; a scribe
was an expert in Jewish religious law. In the NT, scribes are shown arguing
with Jesus on many occasions. CS 259 has τοῦ ἀρχιερέως (*of the high priest*)
in place of τοῦ γραμματέως. ἦν ἑστὼς: periphrastic construction of perf.
part. (with pres. meaning) + the imperf. of the verb εἰμί. ἑστὼς: masc. nom.
sing. perf. act. part. < ἵστημι. ἐξέχεε: 3ʳᵈ sing. aor./imperf. act. indic. < ἐκχέω.

3:2 γινόμενον: Attic prose before *c.* 325 BCE normally uses the γιγν- present-
tense stem of this verb (Ionic and LG use the γιν-stem). πρὸς αὐτόν:
although πρός + acc. pron. with verbs of saying in CG suggests a more
forceful reponse than simply employing a dat. pron., in IGT (cf. 4:1 below) and
other LG texts the two constructions are identical in meaning. Σοδομίτα: by
calling Anna's son a Sodomite, Jesus is simply stating that the boy is, like the
citizens of Sodom (and Gomorrah) in the Old Testament (Genesis 18:1-19:29),
an evil individual damned by God. ὡς: *like.* ἀποξηρανθῇς: 2ⁿᵈ sing.
aor. pass. subju. < ἀποξηραίνω; in LG the subju. can have the force of the fut.,
as here. οὐ μή ἐνέγκῃς: οὐ μή + subju. = an emphatic denial; i.e., *you will
never again...* Jesus' curse on the child is similar to the one he makes on a fig
tree in Mark (11:12-14) and Matthew (21:18-19). Cf. also Psalm 1:3.

Vocabulary

ἀγανακτέω, *be angry*

ἀδικέω, *wrong, injure*

Ἄννα, ὁ, (indecl.) *Annas*

ἀπέρχομαι, ἀπελεύσομαι, ἀπῆλθον, *go, go away, depart*

ἀποξηραίνω, *dry up, scorch*; (pass.) *be completely dried up; wither; become stiff*

ἀνόητος, -ον, *foolish*

ἀσεβής, -ές, *ungodly, godless, unholy*

γί(γ)νομαι, *become*

γραμματεύς, -έως, ὁ, *scribe, expert in the Jewish law; clerk, scholar*

δένδρον, τό, *tree*

διηγέομαι, *describe in full*

ἐκεῖ, adv., *there*

ἐκχέω, (ἐξεχέα, LG aor.) *pour out*

θαμβέω, *be astounded, amazed*

ἰδού, adv., *look!*

Ἰουδαῖος, ὁ, *Judean, Jew*

ἵστημι, στήσω, ἔστησα, *make X stand; stop X; set X (up)*; (2nd aor.)
   ἔστην, (perf.) ἔστηκα, *stand*

ἰτέα, -ας, ἡ, *willow*

καρπός, ὁ, *fruit*

κλάδος, ὁ, *small branch*

λαμβάνω, λήψομαι, ἔλαβον, *take*

λάκκος, ὁ, *pond*

λέγω, ἐρῶ, εἶπον, *say, speak, tell*

νῦν, adv., *now*

ὅσπερ, ἥπερ, ὅπερ, rel. pron., emphatic forms, *who, whose, whom, which, that*

ὁράω, ὄψομαι, εἶδον, *see*

οὔτε...οὔτε, conj., *neither...nor*

πρῶτοι, οἱ, *the leaders*

ποιέω, *make, produce, create; do*

ῥίζα, ἡ, *root*

Σοδομίτης, -ου, ὁ, *Sodomite.*

συνάγω, συνάξω, συνήγαγον, *bring or gather together*

τίς, τί, (gen. τίνος) interrog. pron. and adj., *who? which? what?*

ὕδωρ, ὕδατος, τό, *water*

υἱός, ὁ, *son*

φέρω, οἴσω, ἤνεγκα (CG more often ἤνεγκον), *carry, bring, bear*

φύλλον, τό, *leaf*

³ καὶ εὐθέως ὁ παῖς ἐκεῖνος ἐξηράνθη ὅλος. ὁ δὲ Ἰησοῦς

ἀνεχώρησε καὶ ἀπῆλθεν εἰς τὸν οἶκον Ἰωσήφ. ⁴ οἱ δὲ γονεῖς

τοῦ ξηρανθέντος ἐβάστασαν αὐτὸν θρηνοῦντες τὴν νεότηταν

αὐτοῦ. καὶ ἤγαγον πρὸς τὸν Ἰωσήφ καὶ ἐνεκάλουν αὐτὸν ὅτι

"τοιοῦτον ἔχεις παιδίον ἐργαζόμενον τοιαῦτα."

4. εἶτα πάλιν ἐπορεύετο διὰ τῆς κώμης, καὶ παιδίον τρέχων

διερράγη εἰς τὸν ὦμον αὐτοῦ. καὶ πικρανθεὶς ὁ Ἰησοῦς

εἶπεν αὐτῷ· "οὐκ ἀπελεύσει τὴν ὁδόν σου." ² καὶ παραχρῆμα

πεσὼν ἀπέθανεν.

※※

3:3 ὅλος: predicate adjs. are sometimes best translated into English as advs.
Ἰωσήφ: gen.

3:4 τοῦ ξηρανθέντος: sc. παιδός. ἤγαγον: James, Cullmann, Elliott, and
Ehrman/Pleše translate this in the CG sense and sc. *him*, i.e., the body of their
dead son; Hock translates it in the LG sense. ὅτι: here signals the beginning
of direct discourse and should not be translated. τοιοῦτον...τοιαῦτα:
although IGT is not a sophisticated literary text, the prose occasionally reveals
rhetorical flourishes, such as this use of *epanalepsis*, which is the repetition
of the initial word (or words) of a clause or sentence at the end of that same
clause or sentence. See 6:23 and 15:5 for other examples of rhetorical figures.

4:1 ἐπορεύετο: sc. Jesus as subj. παιδίον τρέχων διερράγη ὦμον
αὐτοῦ: Tischendorf B describes a different action that motivates Jesus'
response: παιδίον τι ῥῖψαν λίθον κατ' αὐτοῦ ἔπληξεν τὸν ὦμον
(*a certain child threw a stone at him and hit his shoulder*). διερράγη:
3ʳᵈ sing. 2ⁿᵈ aor. act. indic. < διαρρήγνυμι. ἀπελεύσει: the fut. of ἔρχομαι
and its compounds in CG Attic is εἶμι; in other CG dialects and in LG, it is
ἐλεύσομαι. καὶ πικρανθεὶς...τὴν ὁδόν σου.": CS 259 is quite
different at this point: καὶ λέγει αὐτῷ ὁ Ἰησοῦς· "ἐπικατάρατός συ ὁ
ἡγεμών σου." (*and Jesus says to him, "Cursed* [sc. be] *your ruling power."*).

Vocabulary

ἄγω, ἄξω, ἤγαγον, (LG) *go*; (CG) *lead, take, bring*

ἀναχωρέω, *go back*

ἀπέρχομαι, ἀπελεύσομαι, ἀπῆλθον, *go, go away, depart*

ἀποθνῄσκω, ἀποθανοῦμαι, ἀπέθανον, *die*

αὐτός, -ή, -ό, (CG, pron. in gen., dat., acc.) *him, her, it, them*; (LG, pron. in all cases) *he, she, it, they*

βαστάζω, *carry off* or *away (a body for burial)*

γονεύς, γονέως, ὁ, *father*; (pl.) *parents*

διαρρήγνυμι, (LG) *bump (hard)*; (CG) *break through, split asunder*

ἐγκαλέω, *accuse*

εἶτα, adv., *then, next*

ἐκεῖνος, -ή, -ό, *that*; (pl.) *those*

ἐργάζομαι, *do, accomplish*; *work*

ἔχω, ἕξω, ἔσχον, *have*; *hold*; (+ inf.) *can, be able, must*; *have* (sc. the power)

εὐθέως, adv., *immediately, at once*

θρηνέω, *lament, sing a funeral song*

κώμη, ἡ, *village*

λέγω, ἐρῶ, εἶπον, *say, speak, tell*

νεότης, νεότητος, ἡ, (LG) *youth*; (CG) *youthful spirit, impetuosity, rashness*

ξηραίνω, *dry up*; (pass.) *become dry*; *wither*; *become stiff*

ὁδός, ὁδοῦ, ἡ, *road, way, journey*

οἶκος, ὁ, *house, home, dwelling*

ὅλος, -η, -ον, *whole, entire*

ὅτι, conj., *that, because*

παιδίον, τό, (diminutive of παῖς, ὁ or ἡ) (LG) *child*; (CG) *little* or *young child*

παῖς, παίδος, ὁ or ἡ, *boy, girl, son, daughter, child*

πάλιν, adv., *again, once more, in turn*

παραχρῆμα, adv., *on the spot, at once*

πικραίνω, *make sharp or bitter to the taste*; (pass.) *feel exasperated, bitter, or angry*

πίπτω, πεσοῦμαι, ἔπεσον, *fall*

πορεύομαι, *go, walk, journey*

τοιοῦτος, τοιαύτη, τοιοῦτο, *such*

τρέχω, δραμοῦμαι, ἔδραμον, *run*

ὦμος, ὁ, *shoulder*

³ ἰδόντες δέ τινες τὸ γινόμενον εἶπον· "πόθεν τοῦτο τὸ

παιδίον ἐγεννήθη, ὅτι πᾶν ῥῆμα αὐτοῦ ἔργον ἐστὶν ἕτοιμον;"

⁴ καὶ προσελθόντες οἱ γονεῖς τοῦ τεθνεῶτος τῷ Ἰωσήφ

κατεμέμφοντο λέγοντες· "σὺ τοιοῦτον παιδίον ἔχων

οὐ δύνασαι μεθ' ἡμῶν οἰκεῖν ἐν τῇ κώμῃ — ἢ δίδασκε αὐτῷ

εὐλογεῖν καὶ μὴ καταρᾶσθαι· τὰ γὰρ παιδία ἡμῶν θανατοῖ."

5. καὶ προσκαλεσάμενος ὁ Ἰωσήφ τὸ παιδίον κατ' ἰδίαν

ἐνουθέτει αὐτὸν λέγων· "ἵνα τί τοιαῦτα κατεργάζει; καὶ

πάσχουσιν οὗτοι καὶ μισοῦσιν ἡμᾶς καὶ διώκουσιν."

×××

4:4 τοῦ τεθνεῶτος: sc. παιδίου. μεθ' ἡμῶν = μετὰ ἡμῶν. σὺ τοιοῦτον παιδίον ἔχων: cf. 3:4 above, τοιοῦτον ἔχεις παιδίον. ἔχων: the part. is used here in a causal sense, i.e., *since you have*. δίδασκε αὐτῷ εὐλογεῖν: CG prefers the construction διδάσκω + acc. + inf. εὐλογεῖν καὶ μὴ καταρᾶσθαι: cf. Romans 12:14: εὐλογεῖτε τοὺς διώκοντας ὑμᾶς, εὐλογεῖτε καὶ μὴ καταρᾶσθε (*bless those persecuting you, bless* [sc. them] *and don't curse* [sc. them]). τὰ γὰρ παιδία, θανατοῖ: neut. pl. subjects normally take sing. verbs in Greek (but cf. IGT 9:1: τὰ ἄλλα παιδία ἔφυγον; LG is often more flexible with respect to neut. pl. subject-verb agreement).

5:1 κατ' ἰδίαν: *in private.* ἵνα τί = ἵνα τί γένηται: literally, *in order that what might happen?*, i.e., *for what purpose* or *reason?*, *why?* κατεργάζει: 2ⁿᵈ sing. pres. act. (dep.) indic. καὶ πάσχουσιν...διώκουσιν: perhaps Joseph's anger and exasperation at young Jesus' behavior explain the unnecessary use of καί at the beginning of this sentence. διώκουσιν: sc. ἡμᾶς.

Vocabulary

ἀποθνῄσκω, ἀποθανοῦμαι, ἀπέθανον, *die*

γεννάω, *be father of, give birth to*; (pass.) *be born*

γί(γ)νομαι, *become*

γονεύς, γονέως, ὁ, *father*; (pl.) *parents*

διδάσκω, *teach*

διώκω, (LG) *persecute*; *drive out* or *away*; (CG) *pursue, chase; prosecute*

δύναμαι, (+ inf.) *be able, can*

ἔργον, τό, *work, deed*

ἕτοιμος, -η, -ον, *carried into effect, already done*

εὐλογέω, (LG) *bless*; (CG) *speak well of, praise, honor*

ἤ, conj., *or*

θανατόω, *die*

ἴδιος, -α, -ον, *private*

καταμέμφομαι, *find great fault with, blame greatly, accuse*

καταράομαι, *call down curses upon, curse*

κατεργάζομαι, *do, accomplish*

κώμη, ἡ, *village*

λέγω, ἐρῶ, εἶπον, *say, speak, tell*

μισέω, *hate*

νουθετέω, *admonish, reprimand*

οἰκέω, *live, dwell*

ὁράω, ὄψομαι, εἶδον, *see*

ὅτι, conj., *that, because*

οὗτος, αὕτη, τοῦτο, *this*; (pl.) *these*

παιδίον, τό, (diminutive of παῖς, ὁ or ἡ) (LG) *child*; (CG) *little* or *young child*

πᾶς, πᾶσα, πᾶν, *all, every, whole*

πάσχω, πείσομαι, ἔπαθον, *suffer*

πόθεν, adv., *from where*

προσέρχομαι, προσελεύσομαι, προσῆλθον, (+ dat.) *approach*

προσκαλέω, *call to, call on*; (mid.) *call to oneself, summon*

ῥῆμα, ῥήματος, τό, *word*

τις, τι, (gen. τινος) indefinite pron., *someone; something; anyone; anything*

τοιοῦτος, τοιαύτη, τοιοῦτο, *such*

² εἶπε δὲ ὁ Ἰησοῦς· "ἐγὼ οἶδα ὅτι τὰ ῥήματα ταῦτα οὐκ

ἐστιν ἐμά, ἅπερ ἐγὼ ἐλάλησα. ὅμως σιγήσω διὰ σέ· ἐκεῖνοι

δὲ οἴσουσιν τὴν κόλασιν αὐτῶν." καὶ εὐθέως οἱ ἐγκαλοῦντες

αὐτὸν ἀπετυφλώθησαν.

³ καὶ οἱ ἰδόντες ἐφοβήθησαν σφόδρα καὶ ἠπόρουν, καὶ

ἔλεγον περὶ αὐτοῦ ὅτι "πᾶν ῥῆμα ὃ ἐλάλει, εἴτε καλὸν εἴτε

κακόν, ἔργον ἦν καὶ θαῦμα ἐγένετο." ⁴ ἰδὼν δὲ ὅτι τοιοῦτον

ἐποίησεν ὁ Ἰησοῦς, ὀργισθεὶς ὁ Ἰωσὴφ ἐπέλαβεν αὐτοῦ τὸ

ὠτίον καὶ ἔτεινεν σφόδρα.

✕✕

5:2 διὰ σέ: *for your sake.* ἀπετυφλώθησαν: as an adult in the NT, Jesus
  heals the blind (Mark 8:22-26, 10:46-52; Matthew 9:27-31, 20:29-34; Luke
  18:35-43; John 9:1-12).
5:3 ὅτι: here signals the beginning of direct discourse and should not be
  translated. ὀργισθεὶς ὁ Ἰωσήφ: this is the reading of Greek-Slav, along
  with the Latin and Syriac versions. Tischendorf A reads: ἐγερθεὶς ὁ Ἰωσήφ
  (*Having gotten up, Joseph...*).

What did Jesus actually say in IGT 5:2?

The text printed above (τὰ ῥήματα ταῦτα οὐκ ἐστιν ἐμά, ἅπερ ἐγὼ
ἐλάλησα) is the reading of Greek-Slav. The three Greek versions that include
Jesus' words are as follows:

  Tischendorf A: τὰ ῥήματά σου ταῦτα οὐκ εἰσὶν σά
      (*these words of yours are not your own*)

  CA 355: τὰ ῥήματα οὐκ ἔστιν ἐμά, ἀλλὰ σά εἰσιν
      (*the words are not my own, but they are your own*)

  CS 259: φρόνιμα ῥήματά συ εἰ γινώσκεις ἄν, πόθεν ἦν τὰ
      ῥήματά σου οὐκ ἀγνοεῖς. ἐπὶ πέπ(=ν?)τε διήγισαν.
      (*since you know wise words, you are not ignorant of where
      your words came from: they were spoken [about a 5-year old?]*)

14

Vocabulary

ἀπορέω, *be at a loss*

ἀποτυφλόω, (LG) *blind, make blind*; (pass.) *be* or *become blind*

ἐγκαλέω, *accuse*

εἴτε...εἴτε, *either...or, whether...or*

ἐκεῖνος, -ή, -ό, *that*; (pl.) *those*

ἐμός, -ή, -όν, *my, mine*

ἐπιλαμβάνω, *lay hold of, seize*

ἔργον, τό, *work, deed*

εὐθέως, adv., *immediately, at once*

θαῦμα, -τος, τό, (LG) *miracle*; (CG) *wonder, marvel*

κακός, -ή, -όν, *bad, evil*

καλός, -ή, -όν, (LG) *good*; (CG) *beautiful, fine*

κόλασις, -εως, ἡ, *punishment*

λαλέω, (LG) *say, speak, tell*; (CG) *talk (aimlessly), chat, babble*

λέγω, ἐρῶ, εἶπον, *say, speak, tell*

οἶδα, (perf. with pres. meaning) *know*

ὅμως, conj., *nevertheless*

ὁράω, ὄψομαι, εἶδον, *see*

ὀργίζω, *make X angry*; (pass.) *grow angry, be angry* or *furious*

ὅς, ἥ, ὅ, rel. pron., *who, whose, whom, which, that*

ὅσπερ, ἥπερ, ὅπερ, rel. pron., emphatic forms, *who, whose, whom, which, that*

ὅτι, conj., *that, because*

οὗτος, αὕτη, τοῦτο, *this*; (pl.) *these*

πᾶς, πᾶσα, πᾶν, *all, every, whole*

ποιέω, *make, produce, create*; *do*

ῥῆμα, ῥήματος, τό, *word*

σιγάω, *be silent*

σφόδρα, adv., *very, very much, strongly, violently*

τείνω, *stretch, pull*

τοιοῦτος, τοιαύτη, τοιοῦτο, *such*

φέρω, οἴσω, ἤνεγκα (CG more often ἤνεγκον), *carry, bring, bear*

φοβέομαι, *be frightened* or *afraid*

ὠτίον, τό, (LG diminutive of οὖς, τό) *ear*

⁵ τὸ δὲ παιδίον ἠγανάκτησε καὶ εἶπεν αὐτῷ· "ἀρκετόν

σοί ἐστιν ζητεῖν καὶ μὴ εὑρίσκειν, καὶ μάλιστα οὐ σοφῶς

ἔπραξας· ⁶ οὐκ οἶδας ὅτι σός; μή με λύπει."

6. διδάσκαλος δέ τις ὀνόματι Ζακχαῖος ἠκροᾶτο πάντα

ὅσα ἐλάλει Ἰησοῦς πρὸς τὸν Ἰωσήφ καὶ ἐθαύμαζε λέγων

ἐν ἑαυτῷ· "τοιοῦτον παιδίον ταῦτα φθέγγεται." ² καὶ

προσκαλεσάμενος τὸν Ἰωσήφ λέγει αὐτῷ· "φρόνιμον

παιδίον ἔχεις καὶ καλὸν νοῦν ἔχει, ἀλλὰ παράδος μοι αὐτὸν

ἵνα μάθῃ γράμματα, καὶ διδάξω αὐτόν πᾶσαν ἐπιστήμην ἵνα

μὴ ᾖ ἀνυπότακτον."

✕✕✕

5:5 ζητεῖν καὶ μὴ εὑρίσκειν: cf. Jesus' words at Matthew 7:7: ζητεῖτε καὶ εὑρήσετε (*seek and you shall find*). CS 259 has ζητεῖν με καὶ εὑρίσκειν.
5:6 οὐκ οἶδας ὅτι σός;: *Don't you know that (I am) yours?* Greek-Slav has οὐκ οἶδας ὅτι σός εἰμι καὶ πρὸς σὲ πάρειμι; (*Don't you know that I am yours and that I'm here with you?*); CA 355 has οὐκ οἶδας τίς εἰμι καὶ πρὸς σὲ πάρειμι; (*Don't you know who I am and that I'm here with you?*); CS 259 has the much longer: *and in addition to this not to beat me severely by having a natural ignorance. You did not see with light why I am yours. Look! You know not to distress me. For I am yours and have been put into your hands.* λύπει: 2ⁿᵈ sing. pres. act. impera.

6:1 ὀνόματι: dat. of respect, i.e., *called* or *named*. ἐν ἑαυτῷ: i.e., *to himself*.
6:2 παράδος: 2ⁿᵈ sing. aor. act. impera. < παραδίδωμι. μάθῃ: 3ʳᵈ sing. aor. act. subju. < μανθάνω. διδάξω...ἀνυπότακτον: this is the reading of CA 355; Tischendorf A has: *I will teach him all knowledge, and how to greet all the elders and honor them as forefathers and fathers, and to love those of his own age.* Tischendorf B has: *I will teach him the scripture, and I will persuade him to bless all men and not to curse them.* διδάξω: in form, either 1ˢᵗ sing. fut. act. indic. or 1ˢᵗ sing. aor. act. subju.; here it is fut. ᾖ: 3ʳᵈ sing. pres. subju. < εἰμί.

Vocabulary

ἀγανακτέω, *be angry*
ἀκροάομαι, *listen to*
ἀνυπότακτος, -ον, (LG) *unruly, insubordinate*
ἀρκετός, -ή, -όν, (LG) *sufficient*
γράμμα, -ατος, τό, *letter*; (pl.) *letters, writing*
διδάσκαλος, ὁ, *teacher*
διδάσκω, *teach*
ἐπιστήμη, ἡ, *knowledge*
εὑρίσκω, εὑρήσω, ηὗρον / εὗρον, *find*
ἔχω, ἕξω, ἔσχον, *have; hold*; (+ inf.) *can, be able, must; have* (sc. the power)
Ζακχαῖος, ὁ, *Zacchaeus*
ζητέω, *seek, look for*
θαυμάζω, *be amazed, wonder at; admire*
ἵνα, conj. + subju., *in order that* (expressing purpose), *so that* (expressing result)
καλός, -ή, -όν, *beautiful, fine*; (LG) *good*
λαλέω, (LG) *say, speak, tell*; (CG) *talk (aimlessly), chat, babble*
λυπέω, *vex, cause grief* or *pain to* X, *injure*; (pass.) *be sad, sorrowful* or
    distressed; grieve
μάλιστα, adv., *most, most of all, very much, especially, too much*
μανθάνω, *learn, understand*
νοῦς, νοῦ, ὁ, *mind*
οἶδα, (perf. with pres. meaning) *know*
ὄνομα, -ατος, τό, *name*
ὅσος, -η, -ον, *as great as, as much as*; (pl.) *as many as*
ὅτι, conj., *that, because*
οὗτος, αὕτη, τοῦτο, *this*; (pl.) *these*
παιδίον, τό, (diminutive of παῖς, ὁ or ἡ) (LG) *child*; (CG) *little* or *young child*
παραδίδωμι, παραδώσω, παρέδωκα, *hand over, give*
πᾶς, πᾶσα, πᾶν, *all, every, whole*
πράττω, *do, act*
προσκαλέω, *call to, call on*; (mid.) *call to oneself, summon*
σός, -ή, -όν, *your*
σοφῶς, adv., *wisely*
τις, τι, (gen. τινος) indefinite adj., *a certain, some, a, an*
τοιοῦτος, τοιαύτη, τοιοῦτο, *such*
φθέγγομαι, *speak, utter*
φρόνιμος, -ον, *wise, sensible, prudent, thoughtful, intelligent*

³ ἀποκριθεὶς δὲ Ἰωσὴφ εἶπεν αὐτῷ· "οὐ δύναταί τις

τοῦτον ὑποτάξαι, εἰ μὴ μόνος θεός· μὴ μικρὸν σταυρὸν

νομίσῃς αὐτον εἶναι, ἀδελφέ."

⁴ ὡς δὲ ἤκουσεν ὁ Ἰησοῦς τοῦ Ἰωσὴφ τοῦτο λέγοντος

ἐγέλασε καὶ εἶπε πρὸς τὸν Ζακχαῖον· "ἀληθῶς, καθηγητά·

ὅσα εἴρηκέ σοι ὁ πατήρ μου ἀληθές ἐστι. ⁵ καὶ τούτων μὲν

ἐγώ εἰμι κύριος καὶ πρὸς σὲ πάρειμι καὶ ἐν ὑμῖν ἐγεννήθην

καὶ μεθ᾽ ὑμῶν εἰμι. ⁶ ἐγὼ οἶδα ὑμᾶς πόθεν ἐστὲ καὶ πόσα ἔτη

ἔσται τῆς ζωῆς ὑμῶν· ἀληθῶς λέγω σοι, διδάσκαλε, ὅτε

ἐγεννήθης ἐγὼ εἰμί· καὶ εἰ θέλεις τέλειος εἶναι διδάσκαλος,

ἄκουσόν μου κἀγὼ διδάξω σε σοφίαν ἣν οὐδεὶς ἄλλος οἶδε

✕✕✕

6:3 εἰ μὴ: *except.* μὴ μικρὸν... εἶναι = μὴ νομίσῃς αὐτον εἶναι μικρὸν
σταυρὸν. μὴ, νομίσῃς: μή + (2ⁿᵈ sing. or pl.) aor. subju. = negative
command. σταυρὸν: as Hock notes (113), "Seemingly an idiomatic
expression for a simple task, but later (v. 8) it is used to refer to Jesus' eventual
crucifixion." CS 259 has μικροῦ ἀνθρώπου (*a little human*) for μικρὸν
σταυρὸν. Aasgaard notes (140) that, "the phrase is ambiguous and can also
be translated "to be almost a man" or "not to be a little man." The meaning
appears to be that Jesus is not only an ordinary human being, but should also be
considered divine. However, it can also mean that the boy has shown himself
so far from being a responsible (adult) person that the challenge will be more
than Zacchaeus can handle."
6:4 ὡς + aor. indic. = *when, after.* εἴρηκέ: 3ʳᵈ sing. perf. act. indic. < λέγω.
6:5 τούτων: sc. ἀνθρώπων. πρὸς σὲ: (LG) *with you,* i.e., in fellowship with
you (cf. John 1:1, καὶ ὁ λόγος ἦν πρὸς τὸν θεόν). μεθ᾽ = μετά.
6:6 εἰμί: *I exist,* i.e., I already existed. θέλεις: CG prose prefers the spelling
ἐθέλεις. κἀγὼ: crasis for καὶ ἐγώ. ἄκουσον: 2ⁿᵈ sing. aor. act. impera.
< ἀκούω.

Vocabulary

ἀδελφός, ὁ, brother

ἀκούω, hear

ἀληθή, -ές, true, truthful

ἀληθῶς, truly, in truth

ἀλλός, -ή, -ό, another, other

ἀποκρίνομαι, answer, reply; (aor. pass. ἀπεκρίθην, ἀποκριθῆναι, and ἀποκριθείς, which first appear in LG, have the same meaning as the CG mid.)

αὐτός, -ή, -ό, (CG, pron. in gen., dat., acc.) him, her, it, them; (LG, pron. in all cases) he, she, it, they

γελάω, laugh

γεννάω, γεννήσω, be father of, give birth to; (pass.) be born

διδάσκαλος, ὁ, teacher

δύναμαι, (+ inf.) can, be able to

ἔτος, -ους, τό, year

ζωή, -ῆς, ἡ, life

θέλω, (+ inf.) wish, desire, want

θεός, ὁ, God

καθηγητής, -οῦ, ὁ, (LG) teacher

κύριος, ὁ, (LG) Lord (title of God in the Old Testament and of Jesus Christ in the New Testament); (CG) lord, master, head (of a family/household); sir

μικρός, -ά, -ό, little, small

μόνος, -η, -ον, only, alone

νομίζω, think, suppose, assume

οἶδα, (perf. with pres. meaning) know

ὅς, ἥ, ὅ, rel. pron., who, whose, whom, which, that

ὅσος, -η, -ον, as great as, as much as; (pl.) as many as

ὅτε, conj., when

οὐδείς, οὐδεμία, οὐδέν, no one, nothing; no

οὗτος, αὕτη, τοῦτο, this; (pl.) these

πάρειμι, (πάρα + εἰμί) be present or here; be present so as to help; have come

πατήρ, πατρός, ὁ, father

πόθεν, adv., from where

πόσος, -η, -ον, how much, how many

σοφία, ἡ, wisdom, insight, intelligence, knowledge

σταυρός, ὁ, cross

τέλειος, -α, -ον, complete, perfect

τις, τι, (gen. τινος) indefinite pron., someone; something; anyone; anything

ὑποτάσσω, rule, control, subordinate; (pass.) be obedient to, obey

---

19

πλὴν ἐμοῦ καὶ τοῦ πέμψαντός με πρὸς ὑμᾶς. [7] σὺ γὰρ

τυγχάνεις ἐμὸς μαθητὴς κἀγὼ οἶδά σε πόσων ἐτῶν εἶ καὶ

πόσον ἔχεις ζῆσαι. [8] καὶ ὅταν ἴδῃς τὸν σταυρόν μου ὃν

εἶπεν ὁ πατήρ μου, τότε πιστεύσεις ὅτι πάντα ὅσα εἶπόν

σοι ἀληθῆ εἰσιν."

[9] οἱ δὲ παριόντες Ἰουδαῖοι καὶ ἀκούοντες τὸν Ἰησοῦν

ἐθαύμασαν καὶ εἶπον· "ὦ ξένον καὶ παράδοξον πρᾶγμα·

οὔπω ἐστὶν ἐτῶν πέντε τὸ παιδίον τοῦτο καὶ τοιαῦτα

φθέγγεται· τοιούτους γὰρ λόγους οὐδέποτε ἠκούσαμεν

εἰρηκότος τινὸς ὡς τὸ παιδίον τοῦτο."

✕✕

6:6 τοῦ πέμψαντός με: this expression is repeatedly used in John's gospel (4:34, 5:24,37, 6:44, 7:16; 8:26, etc.), and signals that the text has shifted to what scholars call a high Christological level (see text box below).
6:7 τυγχάνεις: sc. ὤν. πόσον: sc. χρόνον.
6:8 ἴδῃς: 2nd sing. aor. act. subju. < ὁράω. εἰσιν: when the subj. is neut. pl., CG prefers to use a sing. verb (ἐστιν).
6:9 εἰρηκότος: gen. masc. sing. perf. act. part. < λέγω. ὡς: *like*.

Christology

Christology is the branch of Christian theology related to the nature, person, and role of Christ. A high Christology (often expressed, for example, in John's gospel) stresses Jesus' divinity, while a low Christology is when Jesus is portrayed as simply human. In the Synoptic tradition, the Christology is quite mixed, for "even though Jesus is portrayed somewhat as a Hellenistic divine man,... there was no sense that he had existed in eternity past, that he was the creator of the universe, or that he was equal to the one true God." (Ehrman, *The New Testament.*[2] New York: Oxford Univ. Press, 2000, 155). The latter three qualities are all examples of a high Christology as found in John.

Vocabulary

ἀκούω, *hear*

ἀληθή, -ές, *true, truthful*

ἀλλός, -ή, -ό, *another, other*

ἔτος, -ους, τό, *year*

ἔχω, ἔξω, ἔσχον, *have; hold*; (+ inf.) *can, be able, must; have* (sc. the power)

ζάω, (unattested hypothetical form) *live, be alive*

θαυμάζω, *be amazed, wonder at; admire*

λόγος, ὁ, *word, speech*

μαθητής, οῦ, ὁ, *student*

ξένος, -η, -ον, *strange, foreign, unusual*

οἶδα, (perf. with pres. meaning) *know*

ὁράω, ὄψομαι, εἶδον, *see*

ὅς, ἥ, ὅ, rel. pron., *who, whose, whom, which, that*

ὅσος, -η, -ον, *as great as, as much as*; (pl.) *as many as* ὅταν

ὅταν (ὅτε + ἄν; + subju.), *when, whenever*

ὅτι, conj., *that, because*

οὐδείς, οὐδεμία, οὐδέν, *no one, nothing; no*

οὐδέποτε, adv., *never*

οὔπω, adv., *not yet*

παράδοξος, -ον, *incredible, unusual*

πάρειμι, (πάρα + εἶμι) *go by, go pass, pass by*

πᾶς, πᾶσα, πᾶν, *all, every, whole*

πατήρ, πατρός, ὁ, *father*

πέμπω, *send*

πέντε, *five*

πιστεύω, *believe*

πλήν, (+ gen.) *except, besides, but*

πόσος, -η, -ον, *how much, how many*

πρᾶγμα, -τος, τό, *matter, thing, affair*

σταυρός, ὁ, *cross*

τις, τι, (gen. τινος) indefinite pron., *someone; something; anyone; anything*

τότε, adv., *then, at that time*

τυγχάνω, *happen* (+ supplementary participle)

φθέγγομαι, *speak, utter*

¹⁰ ἀποκριθεὶς δὲ ὁ Ἰησοῦς λέγει αὐτοῖς· "πάνυ

θαυμάζετε; μᾶλλον δὲ ἐπιστῆτε ἐφ᾽ οἷς εἶπον ὑμῖν· ἀληθῶς

οἶδα καὶ πότε ἐγεννήθητε ὑμεῖς καὶ οἱ πατέρες καὶ τὸ

παράδοξον λέγω ὑμῖν· ὅτε δὴ ὁ κόσμος ἐκτίσθη, ἐγὼ εἰμὶ

καὶ ὁ πέμψας με πρὸς ὑμᾶς."

¹¹ ἀκούσαντες δὲ οἱ Ἰουδαῖοι ὅτι οὕτως λέγει τὸ παιδίον

ἐφιμώθησαν, μὴ δυνάμενοι ἀποκριθῆναι αὐτῷ λόγον.

¹² προσελθὸν δὲ τὸ παιδίον καὶ σκιρτῆσαν αὐτοῖς λέγει·

"ἔπαιξα ὑμᾶς· οἶδα γὰρ ὅτι μικροθαύμαστοί ἐστε καὶ μικροὶ

τοῖς φρονήμασιν."

¹³ ὡς οὖν ἔδοξαν παρηγορεῖσθαι ἐν τῇ παρακλήσει τοῦ

παιδίου, εἶπεν ὁ καθηγητὴς πρὸς τὸν Ἰωσήφ· "ἄγαγε αὐτὸν

εἰς τὸ παιδευτήριον κἀγὼ αὐτὸν διδάξω γράμματα."

✳✳

6:10 ἐπιστῆτε: 2ⁿᵈ pl. aor. impera./subju. < ἐφίστημι. ἐφ᾽ οἷς = ἐπὶ οἷς: *upon* or *on the things which*. εἰμί: *I exist*, i.e., I (already) existed; the high Christological view expressed here is similar to that in various NT writings (e.g., John 1:1-3; Colossians 1:15-16; Hebrews 1:2; Revelations 3:14). ἐκτίσθη: 3ʳᵈ sing. aor. pass. indic. < κτίζω. ὁ πέμψας με πρὸς ὑμᾶς: sc. ἐστιν.
6:11 ἐφιμώθησαν: this is the reading of CS 259; CA 355 has ἐθυμώθησαν (*were furious*), Greek-Slav ἐφοβήθησαν (*were frightened*).
6:12 μικροθαύμαστοί: this is the only appearance of this word in Greek; it is modeled after such words as μικρόθυμος, -ον (*small-minded*). These people are *micro-marvelers*, i.e., those who marvel or are amazed at trifling, unimportant things; those who are easily impressed.
6:13 ὡς + aor. indic. = *when*. ἐν τῇ παρακλήσει: *by the consolation*.

Vocabulary

ἄγω, ἄξω, ἤγαγον, *lead, take, bring*

ἀληθῶς, *truly, in truth*

ἀποκρίνομαι, *answer, reply*; (aor. pass. ἀπεκρίθην, ἀποκριθῆναι, and ἀποκριθείς, which first appear in LG, have the same meaning as the CG mid.)

γεννάω, γεννήσω, *be father of, give birth to*; (pass.) *be born*

γράμμα, -ατος, τό, *letter*; (pl.) *letters, writing*

δή, *indeed; then, therefore, now*

διδάσκω, *teach*

δοκέω, *think, suppose, imagine*

δύναμαι, (+ inf.) *can, be able to*

ἐφίστημι, ἐπιστήσω, ἐπέστησα, *consider, fix one's mind on, give one's attention to*

θαυμάζω, *be amazed, wonder at; admire*

καθηγητής, -οῦ, ὁ, (LG) *teacher*

κόσμος, ὁ, *world, universe*

κτίζω, *create, make*

λόγος, ὁ, *word, speech*

μᾶλλον, adv., *more, much more; rather, instead*

μικροθαύμαστος, -ον, (unattested word) *marveling at trifles, easily impressed*

μικρός, -ά, -ό, *little, small*

οἶδα, (perf. with pres. meaning) *know*

ὅτε, conj., *when*

ὅτι, conj., *that, because*

οὖν, adv., *therefore, then*

οὕτως, adv., *so, thus*

παιδευτήριον, τό, *school*

παίζω, *play; mock, make fun of*

πάνυ, adv., *altogether, very, exceedingly*

παράδοξος, -ον, *incredible, unusual*

παράκλησις, -εως, ἡ, (LG) *consolation*; (CG) *address, exhortation*

παρηγορέω, *comfort, console*

πατήρ, πατρός, ὁ, *father*

πέμπω, *send*

πότε, adv., *when*

προσέρχομαι, προσελεύσομαι, προσῆλθον, *come* or *go to, approach*

σκιρτάω, *spring, leap*

φιμόω, *muzzle, make silent* or *speechless*; (pass.) *be silenced; become speechless*

φρόνημα, -ατος, τό, *way of thinking, mind*

¹⁴ ὁ δὲ Ἰωσὴφ λαβὼν αὐτὸν ἀπὸ τῆς χειρὸς ἤγαγεν

αὐτὸν εἰς τὸ διδασκαλεῖον. ¹⁵ καὶ ἔγραψεν αὐτῷ ἀλφάβητον

καθηγητὴς καὶ ἤρξατο ἐπιτηδεύειν καὶ εἶπε τὸ ἄλφα

πλειστάκις· τὸ δὲ παιδίον ἐσιώπα καὶ οὐκ ἀπεκρίνατο αὐτὸν.

¹⁶ ὀργισθεὶς οὖν ὁ καθηγητὴς ἔκρουσεν αὐτὸν εἰς τὴν

κεφαλήν· τὸ δὲ παιδίον ἀξίως παθὸν εἶπεν αὐτῷ· "ἐγώ σε

παιδεύω μᾶλλον ἢ παιδεύομαι ἀπὸ σοῦ, ὅτι οἶδα γράμματα ἃ

σύ με διδάσκεις καὶ πολλή σου κρίσις ἐστί· καὶ ταῦτά σοί

ἐστιν ὡς χοῦς χαλκοῦς, ὡς κύμβαλον ἀλαλάζον, ἅτινα οὐ

παρέχουσι διὰ τὴν φωνὴν τὴν δόξαν καὶ τὴν σοφίαν.

✕✕✕

6:14 λαβὼν ἀπὸ τῆς χειρὸς: *by the hand*; CG would have written either λαβὼν αὐτὸν τῆς χειρὸς or (more common) λαβόμενος τῆς χειρὸς (which is used at 18:2).

6:15 ἐπιτηδεύειν: normally an intransive verb, ἐπιτηδεύω here must be transitive; i.e., *drill* (sc. him). Cf. 14:2.

6:16 ἀξίως: since the meaning of this adv. is *in a manner worthy of* or *suitable to*; *deservedly*, there are two possible ways in which it can be interpreted in this context: 1. the author is stating that Jesus *deservedly* suffered at the hands of his teacher since he was being a recalcitrant pupil; 2. Jesus suffered the physical punishment inflicted by his teacher *in a manner worthy of* (sc. his divine being), i.e., by not inflicting grievous injury in turn (Hock, for example, translates ἀξίως as *calmly*). Although 2. would seem more attractive to a Christian author, it must be noted that Jesus' temperament so far in terms of injuries done to his person has been one that has a tendency to not turn the other cheek. CS 259 has ἠγανάκτησεν (*became angry*) in place of ἀξίως παθὸν. παιδεύομαι ἀπὸ σοῦ: with the pass. voice, the agent by whom the action is performed is regularly expressed in CG by ὑπό + gen. (which is used at 7:10 below). σοί: CS 259 has ἐμοί. ὡς: *like*. κύμβαλον ἀλαλάζον: a phrase borrowed from Paul's words on the nature of love (1 Corinthians 13:1).

Vocabulary

ἄγω, ἄξω, ἤγαγον, *lead, take, bring*

ἀλαλάζω, *clang, wail loudly*

ἄλφα, τό, (indecl.) *alpha*

ἀλφάβητον, τό, (LG) *alphabet*

ἀξίως, adv., *in a manner worthy of* or *suitable to; deservedly*

ἀποκρίνομαι, *answer, reply;* (aor. pass. ἀπεκρίθην, ἀποκριθῆναι, and ἀποκριθείς, which first appear in LG, have the same meaning as the CG mid.)

ἄρχω, *rule, govern;* (mid.) *begin*

γράμμα, -ατος, τό, *letter;* (pl.) *letters, writing*

γράφω, *write*

διδασκαλεῖον, τό, *school*

διδάσκω, *teach*

δόξα, ἡ, *glory*

ἐπιτηδεύω, *practice;* (LG) *drill*

καθηγητής, -οῦ, ὁ, (LG) *teacher*

κεφαλή, ἡ, *head*

κρίσις, -εως, ἡ, *condemnation, punishment*

κρούω, *strike, hit*

κύμβαλον, τό, *cymbal*

λαμβάνω, λήψομαι, ἔλαβον, *take*

μᾶλλον, adv., *more, much more; rather, instead*

ὀργίζω, *make X angry;* (pass.) *grow angry, be angry* or *furious*

παιδεύω, *instruct, teach*

πάσχω, πείσομαι, ἔπαθον, *suffer*

παρέχω, παρασχήσω, παρέσχον, *produce, bring about, provide*

πλειστάκις, adv., *many times*

πολύς, πολλή, πολύ, *much;* (pl.) *many*

σιωπάω, *be silent*

σοφία, ἡ, *wisdom, insight, intelligence, knowledge*

φωνή, ἡ, *sound, noise*

χαλκοῦς, -ῆ, -οῦν, *made of copper, brass,* or *bronze*

χείρ, χειρός, ἡ, *hand*

χοῦς, ὁ, *pitcher* (holding nearly 3 quarts)

¹⁷ οὐδέ τινος ψυχὴ συνίησι τὴν δύναμιν τῆς σοφίας μου."

¹⁸ παυσάμενος δὲ ἀπὸ τῆς ὀργῆς εἶπε τὰ γράμματα ἀπὸ τοῦ ἄλφα ἕως τοῦ ω μετὰ πολλῆς ὀξύτητος.

¹⁹ ἐμβλέψας δὲ εἰς τὸν καθηγητὴν λέγει αὐτῷ· "σὺ τὸ ἄλφα μὴ εἰδὼς κατὰ φύσιν, τὸ βῆτα πῶς μᾶλλον διδάσκεις; ²⁰ ὑποκριτά, εἰ οἶδας, δίδαξόν με πρῶτον σὺ τὸ ἄλφα καὶ τότε σοι πιστεύω τὸ βῆτα." ²¹ ὁ δὲ ἤρξατο ἐπερωτᾶν τὸν διδάσκαλον περὶ τοῦ πρώτου στοιχείου· καὶ οὐκ ἴσχυσεν εἰπεῖν οὐδέν.

※※※

6:18 παυσάμενος δὲ ἀπὸ τῆς ὀργῆς: in CG would be either παυσάμενος δὲ τῆς ὀργῆς or παυσάμενος δὲ ἐκ τῆς ὀργῆς.

6:19 μὴ εἰδὼς: the part. here is causal, i.e., *since you don't know*; εἰδὼς = masc. nom. sing. perf. (with pres. meaning) act. part. < οἶδα. κατὰ φύσιν: *with respect to its (true) nature or essence.* διδάσκεις: although the pres. tense is possible, CG would normally use the fut. (διδάξεις); cf. also πιστεύω below.

6:20 πιστεύω: CG would use the fut. (πιστεύσω). This could also be a subju. (i.e., I might believe) or an example of LG's use of the subju. as a fut. (cf. ἀποξηρανθῆς at 3:2). τὸ βῆτα: acc. of respect.

6:21 οὐκ, οὐδέν: Greek can employ double negatives; English – excepting colloquial usage – does not. ἴσχυσεν: the subj. is the teacher.

Vocabulary

ἄλφα, τό, (indecl.) *alpha*

ἄρχω, *rule, govern*; (mid.) *begin* (+ inf.)

βῆτα, τό, (indecl.) *beta*

γράμμα, -ατος, τό, *letter*; (pl.) *letters, writing*

διδάσκαλος, ὁ, *teacher*

διδάσκω, *teach*

δύναμις, -εως, ἡ, *power, supernatural power*

ἐμβλέπω, *look straight at*

ἐπερωτάω, *ask*

ἕως, conj., *until, as far as*; (LG, prep. + gen.) *to, until, as far as, throughout, to the point of, for*

ἰσχύω, (LG) *be able, can*; (CG) *be strong, mighty,* or *powerful; prevail*

καθηγητής, -οῦ, ὁ, (LG) *teacher*

μᾶλλον, adv., *more, much more; rather, instead*

ὀξύτης, -τος, ἡ, *quickness*

ὀργή, ἡ, *anger, wrath*

οὐδείς, οὐδεμία, οὐδέν, *no one, nothing; no*

παύω, *stop*; (mid.) *cease from*

πιστεύω, *believe*

πολύς, πολλή, πολύ, *much*; (pl.) *many*

πρῶτον, adv., *first, first of all*

πῶς, adv., *how?, in what manner* or *way?*

σοφία, ἡ, *wisdom, insight, intelligence, knowledge*

στοιχεῖον, τό, *letter, element*

συνίημι, συνήσω, συνῆκα, *understand, comprehend*

τότε, adv., *then, at that time*

ὑποκριτής, οῦ, ὁ, *hypocrite, imposter*

φύσις, -εως, ἡ, *nature, being, essence*

ψυχή, ἡ, *life-force, soul, spirit; mind, understanding*

²² ἀκουόντων δὲ πολλῶν, λέγει πρὸς Ζακχαῖον· "ἄκουε,

διδάσκαλε, καὶ νόει τὴν τοῦ πρώτου στοιχείου τάξιν. ²³ καὶ

πρόσχες ὧδε πῶς ἔχει δύο κανόνας καὶ χαρακτῆρας μέσον

ὀξυσμένους διαμένοντας, συναγομένους, ὑψουμένους,

χορεύοντας, τριστόμους, διστόμους, ἀμαχίμους, ὁμογενεῖς,

παρόχους, ζυγοστόμους, ἰσομέτρους κανόνας ἔχων τὸ ἄλφα."

7. ὡς δὲ ἤκουσεν ὁ διδάσκαλος Ζακχαῖος τὰς τοσαύτας καὶ

τοιαύτας ἀλληγορίας τοῦ πρώτου γράμματος εἰρηκότος

τοῦ παιδός, ἠπόρησεν ἐπὶ τοσαύτην ἀπολογίαν καὶ

διδασκαλίαν αὐτοῦ, ² καὶ εἶπεν τοῖς παροῦσιν· "οἴμοι,

✖✖

6:22 ἀκουόντων δὲ πολλῶν: gen. abs.

6:23 πρόσχες: 2nd sing. aor. act. impera. < προσέχω. ἔχει...ἔχων τὸ
ἄλφα: note the repetition of ἔχω (called an *inclusio*), and the extreme
separation of subj. (τὸ ἄλφα) and verb (ἔχει). Jesus' explanation of the
"nature" of the letter alpha is the single most perplexing passage in IGT.
The difficulties arise both from the fact that the precocious child has invented
words (at least three, perhaps four), whose meanings must be guessed at based
on an etymological analysis of their roots, and from the fact that the words
seem strung together in such a way that conveys only a very loose picture of
what specific instruction Jesus is attempting to impart about the letter alpha.
For more on this perplexing passage, including a possible solution as to its
nature and function, see **Appendix 3: Jesus' Alpha Lesson**.

7:1 ὡς + aor. indic. = *when, after.* ἤκουσεν...τοῦ παιδός = ὁ διδάσκαλος
Ζακχαῖος ἤκουσεν τοῦ παιδός εἰρηκότος τὰς... εἰρηκότος: gen. masc.
sing. perf. act. part. < λέγω. ἐπὶ διδασκαλίαν αὐτοῦ: *at his astounding
defense and teaching of it* (i.e., the first letter's meaning).

Vocabulary

αἰσχύνη, ἡ, shame, disgrace

ἀκούω, hear

ἀλληγορία, ἡ, allegory

ἄλφα, τό, (indecl.) alpha

ἀμάχιμος, -ον, (unattested word) not antagonistic (?)

ἀπολογία, ἡ, defense

ἀπορέω, be at a loss, be perplexed

γράμμα, -ατος, τό, letter; (pl.) letters, writing

διαμένω, stand firm, stand by

διδασκαλία, -ας, ἡ, teaching, instruction

διστόμος, -ον, two-sided, with two corners

δύο, two

ζυγόστομος, -ον, (unattested word) crossbar (?)

ἰσόμετρος, -ον, (LG) of equal measure

κανών, -όνος, ὁ, straight bar or line

μέσος, -η, -ον, middle, in the middle; (μέσον, adv.) in the middle

νοέω, think over, consider; understand

οἴμοι, ah me! poor me!

ὁμογενής, -ές, of the same race, family, or type

ὀξυσμένος, -ον, (unattested word) of sharp strength (?)

πάρειμι, (πάρα + εἰμι) be present

πάροχος, ὁ, (LG) passenger

προσέχω, προσέξω, προσέσχον, pay close attention to

πρῶτος, -η, -ον, first

πῶς, how?, in what way?

στοιχεῖον, τό, letter, element

συνάγω, συνάξω, συνήγαγον, bring together

τάξις, -εως, ἡ, arrangement, order

τοιοῦτος, τοιαύτη, τοιοῦτο, such

τοσοῦτος, -αύτη, -οῦτον, so much, so great; (pl.) so many

τριστόμος, -ον, three-sided, with three corners

ὑψόω, raise up, elevate; exalt

χαρακτήρ, -ῆρος, ὁ, mark, point; distinctive mark, characteristic

χορεύω, dance

ὧδε, adv., in this way, so, thus

ἠπορήθην ὁ τάλας ἐγώ, ἐμαυτῷ αἰσχύνην παρέχων

ἐπισπασάμενος τὸ παιδίον τοῦτο. ³ ἆρον οὖν αὐτό,

παρακαλῶ σε, ἀδελφὲ Ἰωσήφ· οὐ φέρω τὸ αὐστηρὸν τοῦ

βλέμματος αὐτοῦ οὔτε τὸν τρανῆ λόγον αὐτοῦ. ⁴ τοῦτο τὸ

παιδίον γηγενὴς οὐκ ἔστι, τοῦτο δύναται καὶ πῦρ δαμάσαι·

τάχα τοῦτο πρὸ τῆς κοσμοποιίας ἐστὶν γεγεννημένον.

⁵ ποία γαστὴρ τοῦτο ἐβάστασεν, ποία δὲ μήτηρ τοῦτο

ἐξέθρεψεν, ἐγὼ ἀγνοῶ. ⁶ οἴμοι, φίλε, ἐξέστη μου ἡ διάνοια·

⁷ ἠπάτησα ἑαυτόν, ὁ τρισάθλιος ἐγώ· ἠγωνιζόμην ἔχειν

μαθητήν, καὶ εὑρέθην ἔχειν διδάσκαλον.

××

7:2 ἠπορήθην: 1ˢᵗ sing. aor. pass. indic. < ἀπορέω; the pass. often has the same meaning as the act. Since the act. form of ἀπορέω appears in the previous clause (CS 259, though, has the pass.), the use of the pass. here seems simply to be a case of *variatio*. ὁ τάλας ἐγώ: in apposition to the understood subj. of ἠπορήθην; i.e., *wretch that I (am)*; cf. ὁ τρισάθλιος ἐγώ (7:7) below.
7:3 οὐ φέρω: i.e., *I can't bear* or *endure*.
7:4 δύναται καὶ πῦρ δαμάσαι: a perplexing comment since neither in this text nor anywhere in the NT does Jesus exhibit such an ability. Perhaps Zacchaeus is simply offering a hyperbolic comment about the magnitude of Jesus' powers. καὶ: *even*. ἐστὶν γεγεννημένον: *was born*; LG often employs the periphrastic construction of perf. pass. part. + the pres. of the verb εἰμί in place of the perf. mid./pass. indic.
7:5 ποία...ἐξέθρεψεν: cf. Luke 11:27: ἐγένετο δὲ ἐν τῷ λέγειν αὐτὸν ταῦτα ἐπάρασά τις φωνὴν γυνὴ ἐκ τοῦ ὄχλου εἶπεν αὐτῷ, "μακαρία ἡ κοιλία ἡ βαστάσασά σε καὶ μαστοὶ οὓς ἐθήλασας." (*And it happened while he [i.e., Jesus] was saying these things that a woman from the crowd raised her voice and said to him, "Blessed is the womb that carried you and the breasts at which you nursed."*)
7:7 ἑαυτόν = ἐμαυτόν; in LG the 3ʳᵈ pers. sing. reflexive pron. can also be a 1ˢᵗ or 2ⁿᵈ pers. reflexive pron. εὑρέθην: 1ˢᵗ sing. aor. pass. indic. < εὑρίσκω.

Vocabulary

ἀγνοέω (contracted form, ἀγνοῶ), *be ignorant, do not know*

ἀγωνίζομαι, *strive, do one's best*

ἀδελφός, ὁ, *brother*

αἴρω, ἀρῶ, ἦρα, *take, take up, take away, remove*

αἰσχύνη, ἡ, *shame, disgrace*

ἀπατάω, *deceive*

ἀπορέω, *be at a loss, be perplexed*

αὐστηρός, -ά, -όν, *austere, harsh*

βαστάζω, *carry; carry off* or *away*

βλέμμα, -ατος, *look, glance*

γαστήρ, -τρός, ἡ, *womb*

γεννάω, *be father of, give birth to;* (pass.) *be born*

γηγενής, -ές, *earthborn*

δαμάζω, *subdue, tame; control*

διάνοια, ἡ, *mind, understanding*

δύναμαι, (+ inf.) *be able, can*

ἐκτρέφω, ἐκθρέψω, ἐξέθρεψα, *raise, rear (children)*

ἐξίστημι, (2nd aor.) ἐξέστη, (LG) *be amazed* or *astonished; be deranged*

ἐπισπάω, *draw* or *drag after* one; (mid.) *take on*

εὑρίσκω, εὑρήσω, ηὗρον / εὗρον, *find*

κοσμοποιία, ἡ, *creation of the world*

λόγος, ὁ, *word, speech*

μαθητής, οῦ, ὁ, *student*

μήτηρ, μητρός, ἡ, *mother*

οἴμοι, *ah me! poor me!*

οὔτε, conj., *and not, not, nor*

παρακαλέω (contracted form, παρακαλῶ), *beg*

παρέχω, παρασχήσω, παρέσχον, *produce, bring about, provide*

ποῖος, -α, -ον, *what, which; what kind of*

πῦρ, -ος, τό, *fire*

τάλας, τάλαινα, τάλαν, *suffering, wretched*

τάχα, adv., *perhaps*

τρανής, -ές, *piercing, clear, distinct*

τρισάθλιος, -α, -ον, literally, *thrice-miserable, triply-wretched,* i.e., *very miserable* or *wretched*

φέρω, οἴσω, ἤνεγκα (CG more often ἤνεγκον), *carry, bring, bear*

φίλος, ὁ, *friend*

31

⁸ ἐνθυμοῦμαι, φίλοι, τὴν αἰσχύνην, ὅτι γέρων ὑπάρχων ὑπὸ

παιδίου ἐνικήθην. ⁹ καὶ ἔχω ἐκκακῆσαι καὶ ἀποθανεῖν διὰ

τούτου τοῦ παιδός· οὐ δύναμαι γὰρ ἐν τῇ ὥρᾳ ταύτῃ

ἐμβλέψαι εἰς τὴν ὄψιν αὐτοῦ. ¹⁰ καὶ πάντων εἰπόντων

ὅτι ἐνικήθην ὑπὸ παιδίου μικροῦ, τί ἔχω εἰπεῖν; καὶ τί

διηγήσασθαι περὶ ὧν μοι εἶπε κανόνων τοῦ πρώτου

στοιχείου; ἀγνοῶ, ὦ φίλοι· οὐ γὰρ ἀρχὴν καὶ τέλος αὐτοῦ

γινώσκω. ¹¹ τοιγαροῦν ἀξιῶ σε, ἀδελφὲ Ἰωσήφ, ἀπάγαγε

αὐτὸν εἰς τὸν οἶκόν σου. οὗτος τί ποτε μέγα ἐστίν, ἢ θεὸς

ἢ ἄγγελος ἢ τί εἴπω, οὐκ οἶδα."

✕✕

7:8 ἀποθανεῖν: CS 259 adds ἢ φυγεῖν τῆς κώμης (*or have to flee from this village*). διὰ τούτου τοῦ παιδός: διά + gen. = causal, i.e., *because of, on account of*; in CG (and even in LG) διά + acc. = causal; CS 259, e.g., has διὰ τὸ παιδίον τοῦτο.

7:10 πάντων εἰπόντων: gen. abs. τί διηγήσασθαι = τί ἔχω διηγήσασθαι. αὐτοῦ: either *of it* or *of him*; CS 259 omits this word.

7:11 αὐτὸν εἰς τὸν οἶκόν σου: after αὐτὸν CS 259 adds μετὰ σωτηρίας (*with salvation*). εἴπω: 1ˢᵗ sing. aor. act. subju. < λέγω; this is a deliberative subju.

Zacchaeus' Lament (7:2-11)

Zacchaeus' lament is the longest set-piece in IGT and, as Hock (94-5) notes, seems to reflect a practice exercise set before students in the ancient classroom called an ἠθοποιία (*character-making*), in which pupils had to create a rhetorically-inflected speech around a prompt such as, "What might Heracles say after his final labor?" Aasgaard (48) sees "much in common with other ancient stories that ridicule similar figures,.... Indeed, there is a distinct slapstick quality to the episode: the scene is constructed in a way aiming at comic effect."

Vocabulary

ἄγγελος, ὁ, *angel*; (CG) *messenger*

ἀγνοεώ (contracted form, ἀγνοῶ), *be ignorant, do not know*

ἀδελφός, ὁ, *brother*

αἰσχύνη, ἡ, *shame, disgrace*

ἀξιόω, (contracted form, ἀξιῶ) (LG) *ask, request, beg*

ἀπάγω, ἀπάξω, ἀπήγαγον, *lead away*

ἀποθνήσκω, ἀποθανοῦμαι, ἀπέθανον, *die*

ἀρχή, ἡ, *beginning*

βλέπω, *see; look* (*at* or *on*); *be able to see, gain one's sight*

γέρων, -οντος, ὁ, *old man, grown man*

γι(γ)νώσκω, *know, have knowledge of, understand*

διηγέομαι, *tell, relate*

δύναμαι, (+ inf.) *be able, can*

ἐκκακέω, (LG) *be fainthearted, lack courage, despair; grow weary*

ἐμβλέπω, *look straight at, look at*

ἐνθυμέομαι (contracted form, ἐνθυμοῦμαι), *reflect on, ponder, think deeply of*

ἔχω, ἕξω, ἔσχον, *have; hold*; (+ inf.) *can, be able, must; have* (sc. the power)

θεός, ὁ, *God*

κανών, -όνος, ὁ, *straight bar* or *line*

μέγας, μεγάλη, μέγα, *large, great*

μικρός, -ά, -ό, *little, small*

νικάω, *conquer, overcome, defeat*

οἶκος, ὁ, *house, home, dwelling*

ὄψις, -εως, ἡ, *face*

ποτέ, (enclitic particle) *ever*

πρῶτος, -η, -ον, *first*

στοιχεῖον, τό, *letter*

τέλος, -ους, τό, *end*

τίς, τί (gen. τίνος), interrogative pron., *who? which? what? what sort of?*

τοιγαροῦν, *therefore, then, for that very reason then*

ὑπάρχω (= εἰμί), *be*

φίλος, ὁ, *friend*

ὥρα, ἡ, *time*

33

8. τῶν δὲ Ἰουδαίων παραινούντων τῷ Ζακχαίῳ, ἐγέλασε τὸ

παιδίον μέγα καὶ εἶπεν· "νῦν καρποφορείτωσαν τὰ ἄκαρπα,

καὶ βλεπέτωσαν τὰ ἄβλεπτα, καὶ ἀκουέτωσαν οἱ κωφοὶ ἐν

τῇ συνέσει τῆς καρδίας. ² ἐγὼ ἄνωθεν πάρειμι ἵνα τοὺς

κάτω ῥύσωμαι καὶ εἰς τὰ ἄνω καλέσω, καθὼς προσέταξέ

μοι ὁ ἀποστείλας με πρὸς ὑμᾶς."

³ καὶ ὡς τὸ παιδίον κατέπαυσε τὸν λόγον, εὐθέως

ἐσώθησαν οἱ πάντες οἱ ὑπὸ τὴν κατάραν αὐτοῦ πεσόντες.

⁴ καὶ οὐδεὶς ἀπὸ τότε ἐτόλμα παροργίσαι αὐτόν, ὅπως μὴ

καταράσεται αὐτὸν καὶ ἔσται ἀνάπηρος.

✕✕

8:1 τῶν δὲ Ἰουδαίων παραινούντων τῷ Ζακχαίῳ: gen. abs.;
παραινούντων seems somewhat incongruous here; Hock notes (123) that,
"the context seems to require something like παραμυθουμένων ("consoling")."
CS 259 omits the entire clause. μέγα: the neut. sing. acc. adj. can function
as an adv. (in this case modifying ἐγέλασε). καρποφορείτωσαν,
βλεπέτωσαν, ἀκουέτωσαν: 3rd pl. pres. act. imperatives, i.e., let X...
8:2 ἵνα τοὺς κάτω ῥύσωμαι: this is the reading of CA 355 and Greek-Slav;
Tischendorf A has ἵνα αὐτοὺς καταράσομαι (*in order to curse them*). τοὺς
κάτω: *the ones below*. τὰ ἄνω: *the things above, higher things; heaven*(?).
8:3 ὡς + aor. indic. = *when, after*. ἐσώθησαν...πεσόντες: this seems to
include the boy who had emptied Jesus' ponds (3:3), the boy who bumped into
him (4:2), and the parents of the aforementioned boy who were blinded by
Jesus after blaming Joseph for Jesus' actions against their son (5:2).
8:4 ἀπὸ τότε: (LG) *from that point on, after that*. ὅπως: in CG prose,
purpose clauses formed with ὅπως normally take the subju. (in verse, however,
the fut. indic. is quite common); LG prose uses either the subju. or indic. with
no difference in meaning. καταράσεται, ἔσται: an abrupt change of
subj. from Jesus to the οὐδείς of the preceding clause.

Vocabulary

ἄβλεπτος, -ον, *without sight, blind*

ἄκαρπος, -ον, *infertile, barren, unfruitful*

ἀλλός, -ή, -ό, *another, other*

ἀνάπηρος, ὁ, *cripple*

ἄνω, adv., *above*

ἄνωθεν, adv., *from above*

ἀποστέλλω, *send; send out* or *away*

γελάω, *laugh*

εὐθέως, adv., *immediately, at once*

ἵνα, conj. + subju., *in order that* (expressing purpose), *so that* (expressing result)

καθώς, adv., *as, just as*

καλέω, *summon, call in*

καρδία, ἡ, *heart; mind*

καρποφορέω, *bear fruit, be productive*

καταπαύω, *stop, cease, end*

κατάρα, ἡ, *curse*

καταράομαι, *call down curses upon, curse*

κάτω, adv., *down; below, beneath*

κωφός, -ή, -όν, *deaf; dumb, mute*

μέγας, μεγάλη, μέγα, *large, great*

νῦν, adv., *now*

οἶκος, ὁ, *house, home, dwelling*

ὅπως, *that, in order that*

οὐδείς, οὐδεμία, οὐδέν, *no one, nothing; no*

παραινέω, *advise*

πάρειμι, (πάρα + εἰμί) *be present* or *here; be present so as to help; have come*

παροργίζω, *make angry*

πίπτω, πεσοῦμαι, ἔπεσον, *fall*

προστάσσω, *command, order*

ῥύομαι, *save, rescue, deliver*

σύνεσις, -εως, ἡ, *understanding, insight, intelligence*

σώζω, *save, rescue, deliver; cure, make well*

τις, τι, (gen. τινος) indefinite adj., *a certain, some, a, an*

τολμάω, *dare, be brave* or *bold enough*

τότε, adv., *then, at that time*

9. καὶ μεθ᾽ ἡμέρας δέ τινας ἔπαιζεν ὁ Ἰησοῦς ἐπάνω

διστέγου οἴκου καὶ ἕν τῶν παιδίων τῶν παιζόντων μετ᾽

αὐτοῦ πεσὼν ἀπὸ τῆς στέγης κάτω ἀπέθανε· καὶ ἰδόντα

τὰ ἄλλα παιδία ἔφυγον, καὶ κατέστη ὁ Ἰησοῦς μόνος.

² καὶ ἐλθόντες οἱ γονεῖς τοῦ τεθνεῶτος ἐνεκάλουν

τὸν Ἰησοῦν· "ταραχοποιός, σὺ αὐτὸν κατέβαλες."

³ ὁ δὲ Ἰησοῦς ἀπεκρίνατο· "οὐκ ἐγὼ αὐτὸν κατέβαλον,

ἀλλ᾽ ἐκεῖνος ἑαυτὸν κατέβαλε, οὐ γὰρ ἀκριβῶς πράττων

κατεπήδησεν ἀπὸ τοῦ στέγου καὶ ἀπέθανε."

⁴ κατεπήδησεν ὁ Ἰησοῦς ἀπὸ τοῦ στέγου καὶ ἔστη

παρὰ τὸ πτῶμα τοῦ παιδίου, καὶ ἔκραξε φωνῇ μεγάλῃ καὶ

εἶπεν· "Ζῆνον," — οὕτω γὰρ τὸ ὄνομα αὐτοῦ ἐκαλεῖτο —

"ἀναστὰς εἰπέ μοι, ἐγώ σε κατέβαλον;"

⁵ καὶ ἀναστὰς παραχρῆμα εἶπεν· "οὐχί, κύριε, οὐ

κατέβαλες, ἀλλὰ ἀνέστησας."

✗✗✗

9:1 καὶ μεθ᾽ ἡμέρας δέ τινας: beginning a new paragraph with καί is a
feature of some LG texts (IGT, Mark, Revelation), but καί paired with δέ is
unusual (and redundant). ἕν: this neut. nom. sing. is modified by πεσὼν (masc.
nom. sing. part.; CG would have used πεσόν). ἰδόντα: sc. *what had happened*.
9:5 κύριε: as Hock notes (125), this is the only time Jesus is so addressed by a
character in IGT (cf. 1:1 for the author addressing Jesus with this title); in the
canonical gospels Jesus is often addressed by other characters in this way.

Vocabulary

ἀκριβῶς, adv., *carefully, with care*

ἀλλός, -ή, -ό, *another, other*

ἀνίστημι, ἀναστήσω, ἀνέστησα, *make X stand up, raise* X; (LG) *raise* (from the dead); (2ⁿᵈ aor.) ἀνέστην, *stand up, rise*

ἀποθνῄσκω, ἀποθανοῦμαι, ἀπέθανον, τέθνηκα, *die*

ἀποκρίνομαι, *answer, reply*; (aor. pass. ἀπεκρίθην, ἀποκριθῆναι, and ἀποκριθείς, which first appear in LG, have the same meaning as the CG mid.)

δίστεγος, -ον, (LG) *of two stories, two-storied*

εἷς, μία, ἕν, *one*

ἐγκαλέω, *accuse*

ἐπάνω, (+ gen.) *on, upon*

ἔρχομαι, ἐλεύσομαι, ἦλθον, *come, go*

Ζῆνον, ὁ, *Zeno* (a common name in the ancient world; the most famous Zeno being the founder of the Stoic school of philosophy, Zeno of Citium).

ἡμέρα, ἡ, *day*

ἵστημι, στήσω, ἔστησα, *make X stand; stop X; set X (up)*; (2ⁿᵈ aor.) ἔστην, (perf.) ἕστηκα, *stand*

καθίστημι, (2ⁿᵈ aor.) κατέστην, *stand, stand quiet*

καλέω, *call, name*

καταβάλλω, *throw down*

καταπηδάω, *leap down*

κάτω, adv., *down; below, beneath*

κράζω, *cry out, shriek*

κύριος, ὁ, (LG) *Lord* (title of God in the Old Testament and of Jesus Christ in the New Testament); (CG) *lord, master, head* (of a family/household); *sir*

μέγας, μεγάλη, μέγα, *large, great*

μόνος, -η, -ον, *alone, only*

ὄνομα, -ατος, τό, *name*

οὐχί, (emphatic form of οὐ) *not; no, no indeed*

παίζω, *play*

παραχρῆμα, adv., *on the spot, at once*

πίπτω, πεσοῦμαι, ἔπεσον, *fall*

πράττω, *do, act*

πτῶμα, -ατος, τό, *body, corpse*

στέγη, ἡ, *roof*

ταραχοποιός, -όν, (LG) *troublemaking*; ταραχοποιός, ὁ, *troublemaker*

φεύγω, *flee, run away*

φωνή, ἡ, *voice, sound, noise*

⁶ καὶ ἰδόντες ἐξεπλάγησαν. οἱ δὲ γονεῖς τοῦ παιδίου ἐδόξασαν

τὸν θεὸν ἐπὶ τῷ γεγονότι σημείῳ, καὶ προσεκύνησαν τῷ Ἰησοῦ.

10. μετ' ὀλίγας ἡμέρας σχίζων τις ξύλα ἐν τῇ γειτονίᾳ

νεώτερος, ἔπεσεν ἡ ἀξίνη καὶ διέσχισεν τὴν βάσιν τοῦ ποδὸς

αὐτοῦ, καὶ ἔξαιμος γενόμενος ἀπέθνησκεν.

² θορύμου δὲ γενομένου καὶ συνδρομῆς, ἔδραμε καὶ τὸ παιδίον

Ἰησοῦς ἐκεῖ. καὶ βιασάμενος διῆλθεν τὸν ὄχλον, καὶ ἐκράτησεν

τοῦ νεανίσκου τὸν πεπληγοτά πόδαν, καὶ εὐθέως ἰάθη.

³ εἶπε δὲ τῷ νεανίσκῳ· "ἀνάστα νῦν, σχίζε τὰ ξύλα καὶ

μνημόνευέ μου."

⁴ ὁ δὲ ὄχλος ἰδὼν τὸ γεγονὸς προσεκύνησαν τὸ παιδίον,

λέγοντες· "ἀληθῶς πνεῦμα θεοῦ ἐνοικεῖ ἐν τῷ παιδίῳ τούτῳ."

✕✕

9:6 ἐξεπλάγησαν.: between this sentence and the next, CS 259 adds: καὶ λέγει
αὐτῷ ὁ Ἰησοῦς· "καὶ κοιμοῦ." (*And Jesus says to him, "And go to sleep."* [i.e.,
return to being dead]). γεγονότι: neut. dat. sing. perf. act. part. < γίνομαι.
προσεκύνησαν: in CG προσκυνέω takes the acc. (cf. 10:4 below); this is the
same response Jesus often gets after performing a miracle in the NT.

10:1 σχίζων τις...νεώτερος: a LG construction called the pendent nominative;
it is the *logical* rather than the *syntactical* subj. at or near the beginning of a
sentence. Translate as *when/as a certain young man was...*

10:2 θορύμου δὲ γενομένου καὶ συνδρομῆς: gen. abs. πεπληγοτά:
in LG the perf. act. part. of πλήσσω often has a pass. sense. sing. collective

10:4 ὁ δὲ ὄχλος, προσεκύνησαν: substantives denoting persons (especially
the word ὄχλος) may very rarely take pl. verbs. For the same construction, cf.
IGT 15:4, though there ὄχλος is modified by a pl. part.

Vocabulary

ἀξίνη, ἡ, *ax*

ἀληθῶς, *truly, in truth*

ἀνίστημι, ἀναστήσω, ἀνέστησα, *make X stand up, raise X*; (LG) *raise* (from the dead); (2nd aor.) ἀνέστην, *stand up, rise*

ἀποθνήσκω, ἀποθανοῦμαι, ἀπέθανον, τέθνηκα, *die*

βάσις, -έως, ἡ, *foot* (of the body)

βιάζομαι, (mid.) *exercise force, use force, force one's way*; (pass.) *suffer violence*

γειτονία, ἡ, *neighborhood*

γονεύς, -έως, ὁ, *father*; (pl.) *parents*

διασχίζω, *split in two, cut through*

διέρχομαι, διελεύσομαι, διῆλθον, *go or pass through*

δοκέω, *think, suppose, imagine*

ἐκπλήσσομαι, (2nd aor.) ἐξεπλάγην, *be amazed*

ἐνοικέω, *live in*

ἔξαιμος, -ον, (LG) *drained of blood*

εὐθέως, adv., *immediately, at once*

ἡμέρα, ἡ, *day*

θεός, ὁ, *God, god*

θόρυμος, ὁ, *confusion, disturbance*

ἰάομαι, *heal, cure; restore*

κρατέω, (LG) *take hold of*

μνημονεύω, *remember, keep in mind; make mention of*

νεανίσκος, ὁ, *young man*

νεώτερος, -α, -ον, (LG) *young, younger, youngest*

νῦν, adv., *now*

ξύλον, τό, *wood*

ὀλίγος, -η, -ον, *little, small*; (pl.) *few*

ὄχλος, ὁ, *crowd, multitude*

πίπτω, πεσοῦμαι, ἔπεσον, πέπτωκα, *fall*

πλήσσω, *strike*

πνεῦμα, -ατος, τό, (LG) *Spirit* (of God); (CG) *wind, breeze, breath, spirit*

πούς, πόδος, ὁ, *foot* (LG often adds -ν to the 3rd declension acc. sing. ending)

προσκυνέω, *worship, fall down and worship*

σημεῖον, τό, (LG) *miraculous sign, miracle*; (CG) *sign*

συνδρομή, ἡ, *rushing together*

σχίζω, *split, cut, chop*

τις, τι (gen. τινος), indefinite pron., *someone; something; anyone; anything*

τρέχω, δραμοῦμαι, ἔδραμον, *run*

11. ὄντος δὲ αὐτοῦ ἑξαέτους, πέμπει αὐτὸν ἡ μήτηρ αὐτοῦ

ὕδωρ ἀντλῆσαι καὶ φέρειν ἐν τῷ οἴκῳ. λελυκότος δὲ αὐτοῦ

τὴν ὑδρίαν ἐν τῷ ὄχλῳ ² καὶ συγκρούσασα ἡ ὑρδία ἐκλάσθη.

³ ὁ δὲ Ἰησοῦς ἁπλώσας τὸ παλίον ὅπερ ἦν βεβλημένος

ἐγέμισεν αὐτὸ ὕδωρ καὶ ἤνεγκε τῇ μητρὶ αὐτοῦ.

⁴ ἰδοῦσα δὲ ἡ μήτηρ αὐτοῦ τὸ γεγονὸς σημεῖον κατεφίλει

αὐτόν, καὶ διετήρει ἐν αὐτῇ τὰ μυστήρια ἃ ἔβλεπεν αὐτὸν

ποιοῦντα.

12. πάλιν δὲ ἐν καιρῷ τοῦ σπόρου ἐξῆλθεν τὸ παιδίον μετὰ

τοῦ πατρὸς αὐτοῦ ἵνα σπείρει σῖτον εἰς τὴν χώραν αὐτῶν·

καὶ ἐν τῷ σπείρειν τὸν πατέρα αὐτοῦ ἔσπειρε καὶ τὸ παιδίον

Ἰησοῦς ἕνα κόρον σίτου. ² καὶ θερίσας καὶ ἀλωνίσας

※※※

11:1 μήτηρ: the first mention of Jesus' mother in IGT. ὄντος δὲ αὐτοῦ
ἑξαέτους: gen. abs.; CS 259 says Jesus *was about seven years old.*
ἐν τῷ οἴκῳ = (CG) εἰς τὸν οἶκον. λελυκότος δὲ αὐτοῦ: gen. abs.
11:2 καὶ: is superfluous here. συγκρούσασα: sc. the ground.
11:3 ἦν βεβλημένος: 3rd sing. pluperf. mid. indic. < βάλλω. ἐγέμισεν: in CG
one *fills* X (acc.) *with* Y (gen.); in LG one often finds the double acc. construction.
11:4 διετήρει...ποιοῦντα: recalls what is said of Mary at Luke 2:19, 51. In
place of this clause, CS 259 has: *saying, "Lord, my God, bless my child." For
they feared that someone might slander/be envious of him.* ἐν αὐτῇ: *to herself.*

12:1 σπείρει = σπείρῃ: because of phonetic similarity, subju. verbal endings in
LG are sometimes spelled the same as indic. endings. ἐν τῷ σπείρειν τὸν
πατέρα αὐτοῦ: ἐν τῷ + inf. is a type of articular inf. most often used to
express contemporaneous time; i.e., *while his father was sowing* (sc. σῖτον).

Vocabulary

ἀλωνίζω, (LG) *thresh; work on a threshing-floor*

ἀντλέω, *draw water*

ἀπλόω, *unfold, stretch out*

βάλλω, *throw, hit;* (mid.) *put about oneself, wear*

βλέπω, *see; look (at or on); be able to see, gain one's sight*

γεμίζω, *fill*

διετηρέω, *keep, keep faithfully*

ἐξαετής, -ές, *six years old*

ἐξέρχομαι, ἐξελεύσομαι, ἐξῆλθον, *go out*

θερίζω, *reap, harvest, gather*

ἵνα, conj. + subju., *in order that* (expressing purpose), *so that* (expressing result)

καιρός, ὁ, *time, appointed* or *proper time, season*

καταφιλέω, *kiss*

κλάω, *break*

κόρος, ὁ, *cor* (a dry measure of around 10-12 bushels)

λύω, *release*

μήτηρ, μητρός, ἡ, *mother*

μυστήριον, τό, *secret, mystery*

οἶκος, ὁ, *house, home, dwelling*

ὄχλος, ὁ, *crowd, multitude*

πάλιν, adv., *again, once more, in turn*

παλίον, τό, (LG, loan word from Latin; more often spelled πάλλιον) *cloak*

πέμπω, *send*

σημεῖον, τό, (LG) *miraculous sign, miracle;* (CG) *sign*

σῖτος, ὁ, *grain, wheat*

σπείρω, *sow*

σπόρος, ὁ, *sowing*

συγκρούω, *strike* or *crash together, collide* or *come into collision with*

ὑδρία, ἡ, *water jug*

ὕδωρ, ὕδατος, τό, *water*

φέρω, οἴσω, ἤνεγκα (CG more often ἤνεγκον), *carry, bring, bear*

χώρα, ἡ, *land*

ἐποίησε κόρους ἑκατόν, ³ καὶ καλέσας πάντας τοὺς πτωχοὺς

τῆς κώμης εἰς τὴν ἅλωνα ἐχαρίσατο αὐτοῖς τὸν σῖτον· καὶ

Ἰωσὴφ ἔφερεν τὸ καταλειφθὲν τοῦ σίτου. ⁴ ἦν δὲ ἐτῶν ὀκτὼ

ὅτε τοῦτο ἐποίησε τὸ σημεῖον.

13. ὁ δὲ πατὴρ αὐτοῦ τέκτων ἦν, καὶ ἐποίει ἐν τῷ καιρῷ

ἐκείνῳ ἄροτρα καὶ ζυγούς. ἐπετάγη αὐτῷ κράββατος παρά

τινος πλουσίου ὅπως ποιήσει αὐτῷ. ² τοῦ δὲ ἑνὸς κανόνος

τοῦ καλουμένου ἐναλλάκτου ὄντος κολοβωτέρου, μὴ

ἔχοντ<ο>ς <τοῦ Ἰωσήφ> τ<ι> ποιῆσαι, εἶπεν τὸ παιδίον

ὁ Ἰησοῦς τῷ πατρὶ αὐτοῦ Ἰωσήφ, "θὲς κάτω τὰ δύο ξύλα,

καὶ ἐκ τοῦ σοῦ μέρους ἰσοποίησον αὐτά."

³ καὶ ἐποίησεν Ἰωσὴφ καθὼς εἶπεν αὐτῷ τὸ παιδίον.

⤫⤫

12:3 ἔφερεν: sc. back to his house/storeroom. καταλειφθὲν: neut. acc. sing. aor. pass. part. < καταλείπω.

13:1 ἐπετάγη: 3rd sing. 2nd aor. pass. indic. < ἐπιτάσσω; more common is the first aor. pass. ἐπετάχθη. αὐτῷ, αὐτῷ: i.e., respectively, Joseph, the rich man. παρά: *from, by.* ποιήσει: sc. *it* (i.e., the bed). ποιήσει is either 3rd sing. fut. act. indic. or (LG spelling, cf. σπείρει at 12:1) 3rd sing. aor. act. subju.

13:2 τοῦ δὲ ἑνὸς...ὄντος κολοβωτέρου: gen. abs. κανόνος: here = *board* (of wood). ἐναλλάκτου: although this word is unattested outside of IGT, given the context and the root (e.g., the adv. ἐναλλάξ = *crosswise*), *crossbeam* is a secure conjecture. κολοβωτέρου: sc. *than the others.* μὴ ἔχοντ<ο>ς <τοῦ Ἰωσήφ> τ<ι> ποιῆσαι: gen. abs.; the supplements are those of Hock. θὲς: 2nd sing. aor. act. imp. < τίθημι. ἰσοποίησον: an invented verb, based on the phrase ἴσον ποιέω (cf. 13:3: ἴσον ἐποίησεν).

Vocabulary

ἄλων, -ος, ἡ, *threshing floor*
ἄροτρον, τό, *plow*
δύο, *two*
εἷς, μία, ἕν, *one*
ἑκατόν, *one hundred*
ἐναλλάκτος, ὁ,* (unattested) *crossbeam* (?)
ἐπιτάσσω, *order, command*
ἔτος, -ους, τό, *year*
ζυγός, ὁ, *yoke*
ἰσοποιέω, (unattested) *make equal*
καλέω, *summon, call*
καθώς, adv., *as, just as*
κανών, -όνος, ὁ, *straight bar* or *line.*
καταλείπω, *leave, leave behind*; (pass. often =) *remain*
κάτω, adv., *down; below*
κολοβός, -όν, *short*
κόρος, ὁ, *cor* (a dry measure of around 10-12 bushels)
κράββατος, ὁ, (LG; a [Macedonian?] loan word) *bed, cot*
κώμη, ἡ, *village*
μέρος, -ους, τό, (LG) *place, side; end; part*
μέσος, -η, -ον, *middle, in the middle*
ξύλον, τό, *wood*; here = *piece of wood*
ὀκτώ, *eight*
ὅπως, *that, in order that*
ὅτε, adv., *when*
πατήρ, πατρός, ὁ, *father*
πλουσίος, -α, -ον, *rich*
πτωχός, -ή, -όν, *poor*
σημεῖον, τό, (LG) *miraculous sign, miracle*; (CG) *sign*
σῖτος, ὁ, *grain, wheat*
τέκτων, -όνος, ὁ, *carpenter, builder*
τίθημι, θήσω, ἔθηκα, *put, place, lay, set*
φέρω, οἴσω, ἤνεγκα (CG more often ἤνεγκον), *carry, bring, bear*
χαρίζομαι, *give generously* or *freely*

ἔστη δὲ ὁ Ἰησοῦς ἐκ τοῦ ἑτέρου μέρους καὶ ἐκράτησεν

τὸ κολοβώτερον ξύλον, καὶ ἐκτείνας αὐτὸ ἴσον ἐποίησεν

τοῦ ἄλλου.

⁴ καὶ εἶδεν ὁ πατὴρ αὐτοῦ Ἰωσὴφ καὶ ἐθαύμασε, καὶ

περιλαβὼν τὸ παιδίον κατεφίλει λέγων· "μακάριός εἰμι,

ὅτι τὸ παιδίον τοῦτο δέδωκέ μοι ὁ θεός."

14. ἰδὼν δὲ Ἰωσὴφ τὴν προθυμίαν τοῦ παιδίου καὶ τὴν

ἡλικίαν καὶ τὸν νοῦν, ὅτι ἀκμάζει, πάλιν ἐβουλεύσατο μὴ

εἶναι αὐτὸ ἄπειρον τῶν γραμμάτων, καὶ ἀπαγαγὼν αὐτὸ

παρέδωκεν ἑτέρῳ διδασκάλῳ. ² εἶπε δὲ ὁ διδάσκαλος τῷ

Ἰωσήφ· "πρῶτον παιδεύσω αὐτὸ τὰ ἑλληνικά, ἔπειτα τὰ

ἑβραϊκά." ᾔδει γὰρ ὁ διδάσκαλος τὴν πεῖραν τοῦ παιδίου,

×××

13:3 ἔστη: 3rd sing. 2nd aor. act. indic. < ἵστημι. ἴσον: in CG ἴσος takes the dat.

14:1 ἐβουλεύσατο μὴ εἶναι αὐτὸ ἄπειρον = ἐβουλεύσατο αὐτὸ μὴ εἶναι ἄπειρον. αὐτὸ: i.e., Jesus, the subj. of the indirect statement.

14:2 τὰ ἑλληνικά, τὰ ἑβραϊκά: in both cases sc. γραμμάτα. Quintilian (*c.* 35 - *c.* 100), a Roman writer and educational theorist, recommended that Roman boys should learn Greek before Latin (*Institutio Oratoria* 1.1.12). Most Jews in Palestine in the first century CE were not taught Hebrew. To learn how to read and write τὰ ἑβραϊκά at this time normally meant Aramaic, the spoken and (for the literate) written language of the majority of people in Palestine from *c.* 500 BCE to *c.* 100 CE. But even more important, especially for social mobility, was to learn Greek, the "prestige" language of politics, culture and commerce in the Near East from *c.* 300 BCE to *c.* 500 CE. ᾔδει: 3rd sing. pluperf. (=imperf.) act. indic. < οἶδα. τὴν πεῖραν τοῦ παιδίου: sc. with his previous teacher.

Vocabulary

ἀκμάζω, *be at full bloom, be at one's prime* or *perfection, flourish*

ἀπάγω, ἀπάξω, ἀπήγαγον, *lead away*

ἄπειρος, -ον, *ignorant*

βουλεύω, *plan, decide; deliberate, consider;* (mid.) *determine, resolve*

δίδωμι, δώσω, ἔδωκα, *give*

ἐβραϊκός, -ή, -όν, *Hebrew, Aramaic*

ἐκτείνω, *stretch out, extend*

ἑλληνικός, -ή, -όν, *Greek*

ἔπειτα, adv., *then, afterwards, next*

ἕτερος, -α, -ον, *other, another*

ἡλικία, ἡ, *age*

θαυμάζω, *be amazed, wonder at; admire*

ἴσος, -η, -ον, *equal, the same*

ἵστημι, στήσω, ἔστησα, *make X stand; stop X; set X (up);* (2nd aor.)
    ἔστην, (perf.) ἔστηκα, *stand*

καταφιλέω, *kiss*

κολοβός, -όν, *short*

κρατέω, (LG) *take hold of*

μακάριος, -α, -ον, *blessed, fortunate, happy*

νοῦς, νοῦ, ὁ, *mind*

ξύλον, τό, *wood;* here = *piece of wood*

μέρος, -ους, τό, (LG) *place, side; part*

παιδεύω, *instruct, teach*

πάλιν, adv., *again, once more, in turn*

παραδίδωμι, παραδώσω, παρέδωκα, *hand* or *give over; entrust, commit,*
    give

πεῖρα, ἡ, *experience*

περιλαμβάνω, *embrace*

προθυμία, ἡ, *willingness, readiness, eagerness, zeal*

πρῶτον, adv., *first, first of all*

καὶ ἐφοβήθη αὐτό· ὅμως γράψας τὸν ἀλφάβητον ἐπετήδευεν

αὐτὸ ἐπὶ πολλὴν ὥραν, καὶ οὐκ ἀπεκρίνατο αὐτῷ.

3 εἶπε δὲ αὐτῷ ὁ Ἰησοῦς· "εἰ ὄντως διδάσκαλος εἶ, καὶ εἰ

οἶδας καλῶς τὰ γράμματα, εἰπέ μοι τοῦ ἄλφα τὴν δύναμιν,

κἀγώ σοι ἐρῶ τὴν τοῦ βῆτα."

4 πικρανθεὶς δὲ ὁ διδάσκαλος ἔκρουσεν αὐτὸν εἰς τὴν

κεφαλήν. ὁ δὲ Ἰησοῦς ἀγανακτήσας κατηράσατο αὐτόν.

καὶ εὐθέως ἐλιποθύμησε καὶ ἔπεσεν χαμαὶ ἐπὶ πρόσωπον.

5 ἀπεστράφη δὲ τὸ παιδίον εἰς τὸν οἶκον Ἰωσήφ.

Ἰωσὴφ δὲ ἐλυπήθη, καὶ παρήγγειλε τῇ μητρὶ αὐτοῦ "ὅπως

ἔξω τῆς θύρας μὴ ἀπολύσεις αὐτόν, διότι ἀποθνήσκουσιν

οἱ παροργίζοντες αὐτόν."

✖✖

14:2 ἐπετήδευεν: normally an intransive verb, ἐπιτηδεύω here must be
transitive; i.e., *drill*; cf. 6:15, where the direct object of the verb, αὐτὸ, must
be supplied. ἐπὶ + acc. (temporal) = *for, over a period of.*

14:3 κἀγώ: crasis for καὶ ἐγώ. τὴν τοῦ βῆτα = τὴν δύναμιν τοῦ βῆτα.
For all of 14:3, cf. 6:20.

14:4 πικρανθεὶς δὲ ὁ διδάσκαλος ἔκρουσεν αὐτὸν εἰς τὴν
κεφαλήν: cf. the previous teacher's identical action at 6:16: ὀργισθεὶς οὖν
ὁ καθηγητὴς ἔκρουσεν αὐτὸν εἰς τὴν κεφαλήν. There, however, the
teacher hit Jesus because he had *not* uttered a sound. ἐλιποθύμησε: CS 259
has ἀπέθανεν (*he died*).

14:5 ἀπεστράφη: 3rd sing. 2nd aor. pass. indic. < ἀποστρέφω. τὸν οἶκον
Ἰωσήφ: Ἰωσήφ is gen. ὅπως, μὴ ἀπολύσεις: ὅπως and ὅπως μὴ +
the fut. are used in urgent exhortations and prohibitions, and can be translated
just like the impera., i.e., *Don't let him go.*

Vocabulary

ἀγανακτέω, *be angry*

ἄλφα, τό, (indecl.) *alpha*

ἀλφάβητον, τό, (LG) *alphabet*

ἀποθνήσκω, ἀποθανοῦμαι, ἀπέθανον, *die*

ἀποκρίνομαι, *answer, reply*; (aor. pass. ἀπεκρίθην, ἀποκριθῆναι, and ἀποκριθείς, which first appear in LG, have the same meaning as the CG mid.)

ἀπολύω, *send away, let go, set free, release*

ἀποστρέφω, *turn* one *away, put to flight*; (mid./pass.) *turn back, return*

βῆτα, τό, (indecl.) *beta*

γράφω, *write*

διότι, *because*

δύναμις, -εως, ἡ, *power, supernatural power*

ἔξω, adv., *out, outside*; (+ gen.) *outside, out of*

ἐπιτηδεύω, *practice*; (LG) *drill*

θύρα, ἡ, *door*

καλῶς, adv., *well; rightly, correctly*

καταράομαι, *call down curses upon, curse*

κεφαλή, ἡ, *head*

κρούω, *strike, hit*

λιποθυμέω, *lose consciousness, pass out*

λυπέω, *vex, cause grief* or *pain to* X, *injure*; (pass.) *be sad, sorrowful* or *distressed; grieve*

ὅμως, conj., *nevertheless*

ὄντως, adv., *really, certainly, indeed*; (used as attributive adj.) *real*

παραγγέλλω, παραγγελῶ, παρήγγειλα, *order, command*

παροργίζω, *make angry*

πικραίνω, *make sharp* or *bitter to the taste*; (pass.) *feel exasperated, bitter*, or *angry*

πίπτω, πεσοῦμαι, ἔπεσον, πέπτωκα, *fall*

πολύς, πολλή, πολύ, *much*; (pl.) *many*

πρόσωπον, τό, *face*

φοβέομαι, *fear, be afraid of*

χαμαί, adv., *on* or *to the ground*

ὥρα, ἡ, *time*

15. μετὰ δὲ χρόνον τινὰ ἕτερος πάλιν καθηγητής, γνήσιος

φίλος ὢν τοῦ Ἰωσήφ, εἶπεν αὐτῷ· "ἄγαγέ μοι τὸ παιδίον

εἰς τὸ παιδευτήριον· ἴσως ἂν δυνηθῶ ἐγὼ μετὰ κολακείας

διδάξαι αὐτὸ τὰ γράμματα."

² καὶ εἶπεν Ἰωσήφ· "εἰ θαρρεῖς, ἀδελφέ, ἔπαρον αὐτὸ

μετὰ σεαυτοῦ." καὶ λαβὼν αὐτὸ μετ' αὐτοῦ μετὰ φόβου καὶ

ἀγῶνος πολλοῦ, τὸ δὲ παιδίον ἡδέως ἐπορεύετο.

³ καὶ εἰσελθὼν θρασὺς εἰς τὸ διδασκαλεῖον εὗρε βιβλίον

κείμενον ἐν τῷ ἀναλογίῳ, καὶ λαβὼν αὐτὸ οὐκ ἀνεγίνωσκε τὰ

γράμματα τὰ ἐν αὐτῷ, ἀλλὰ ἀνοίξας τὸ στόμα αὐτοῦ ἐλάλει

πνεύματι ἁγίῳ, καὶ ἐδίδασκε τὸν νόμον τοὺς περιεστῶτας.

✕✕

15:1 δυνηθῶ: 1st sing. aor. pass. (dep.) subju. < δύναμαι.
15:2 ἔπαρον: 2nd sing. aor. act. impera. < ἐπαίρω.
15:3 εἰσελθών: sc. Jesus. θρασὺς: adj. used adverbially (cf. 3:3). πνεύματι
ἁγίῳ: instrumental dat.: *by (the power of) the Holy Spirit*; this is the first explicit
mention in IGT of the third member of the Christian concept of the godhead as
a trinity, though earlier at 10:4 it was stated by the crowd that πνεῦμα θεοῦ
ἐνοικεῖ ἐν τῷ παιδίῳ τούτῳ. ἐδίδασκε τὸν νόμον τοὺς περιεστῶτας:
CA 355 offers an expanded – and slightly different – take at this point: ἐδίδασκε
τὸν νόμον αὐτοῦ τοὺς παρόντας καὶ ἀκούοντας ὥστε καὶ ὁ καθηγητὴς
πλησίον αὐτοῦ καθίσας πάνυ ἡδέως αὐτοῦ ἤκουσεν, παρακαλῶν αὐτὸν
ἵνα πλείονα εἴπῃ (*he was teaching his own law to those who were present and
listening, with the result that even the teacher, who had sat down near him,
listened to him with much pleasure, urging him to say more*). CS 259 is similar
to CA 355, but in place of ἐδίδασκε τὸν νόμον...ἀκούοντας, has ἐπεφθέγξατο
ῥήματα φοβερὰ (*he uttered [such] awe-inspiring [or fearful] words*).
περιεστῶτας: masc. acc. pl. perf. act. part. < περιίστημι. For all of 15:3,
cf. Luke 4:16-17, a similar set of events, though there Jesus is an adult.

Vocabulary

ἁγίος, -α, -ον, *holy*

ἄγω, ἄξω, ἤγαγον, *lead, take, bring*

ἀγών, -ῶνος, ὁ, *concern, trepidation; struggle, fight, contest*

ἀδελφός, ὁ, *brother*

ἀναγι(γ)νώσκω, *read (aloud)*

ἀναλογίος, ὁ, (Medieval Greek word not attested before the 10th century) *desk*

ἀνοίγω (LG form of ἀνοίγνυμι; three aor. forms occur in LG: ἀνέῳξα, ἠνέῳξα, ἤνοιξα), *open*

βιβλίον, τό, *roll, scroll, book*

γνήσιος, -α, -ον, *legitimate, real, true, loyal*

διδασκαλεῖον, τό, *school*

δύναμαι, (+ inf.) *can, be able to*

εἰσέρχομαι, εἰσελεύσομαι, εἰσῆλθον, *enter, go in*

ἐπαίρω, ἐπαρῶ, ἐπῆρα, (LG) *take, take away*; (CG) *lift, raise (up)*

ἕτερος, -α, -ον, *other, another*

εὑρίσκω, εὑρήσω, ηὗρον / εὗρον, *find*

ἡδέως, adv., *gladly*

θαρρέω, *be full of courage, act boldly, be confident*

θρασύς, -εῖα, -ύ, *bold, spirited, courageous*

ἴσως, adv., *perhaps*

κεῖμαι, κείσομαι, *lie*

κολακεία, ἡ, *flattery*

λαλέω, (LG) *say, speak, tell*; (CG) *talk (aimlessly), chat, babble*

λαμβάνω, λήψομαι, ἔλαβον, *take*

νόμος, ὁ, (LG) *law* (i.e., the Jewish sacred tradition, as found, e.g., in the Old Testament); (CG) *custom, usage, law; pasture; province, district*

παιδευτήριον, τό, *school*

πάλιν, adv., *again, once more, in turn*

περιίστημι, περιστήσω, περιέστησα, (LG) *stand around*

πνεῦμα, -ατος, τό, (LG) *Spirit* (of God); (CG) *wind, breeze, breath, spirit*

πορεύομαι, *go, walk, journey*

στόμα, -τος, τό, *mouth*

τις, τι, (gen. τινος), indefinite adj., *a certain, some, a, an*

φίλος, ὁ, *friend*

φόβος, ὁ, *fear*

χρόνος, ὁ, *time*

⁴ ὄχλος δὲ πολὺς συνελθόντες παριστήκεισαν

ἀκούοντες αὐτοῦ, καὶ ἐθαύμαζον ἐν τῇ ὡραιότητι τῆς

διδασκαλίας αὐτοῦ καὶ τῇ ἑτοιμασίᾳ τῶν λόγων αὐτοῦ,

ὅτι νήπιον ὢν τοιαῦτα φθέγγεται.

⁵ ἀκούσας δὲ Ἰωσὴφ ἐφοβήθη, καὶ ἔδραμεν εἰς τὸ

διδασκαλεῖον λογισάμενος μὴ οὗτος ὁ καθηγητής ἐστιν

ἄπειρος.

⁶ εἶπε δὲ ὁ καθηγητὴς τῷ Ἰωσήφ· "ἵνα εἰδῇς, ἀδελφέ, ὅτι

ἐγὼ μὲν παρέλαβον τὸ παιδίον ὡς μαθητήν, αὐτὸ δὲ πολλῆς

χάριτος καὶ σοφίας μεστόν ἐστιν· καὶ λοιπὸν ἀξιῶ σε,

ἀδελφέ, ἆρον αὐτὸ εἰς τὸν οἶκόν σου."

⁷ ὡς δὲ ἤκουσεν τὸ παιδίον ταῦτα, εὐθέως προσεγέλασεν

αὐτῷ καὶ εἶπεν, "ἐπειδὴ ὀρθῶς ἐλάλησας καὶ ὀρθῶς

✳✳✳

15:4 ὄχλος, συνελθόντες παριστήκεισαν ἀκούοντες, ἐθαύμαζον: sing. collective substantives denoting persons (especially the word ὄχλος) may very rarely take pl. verbs (though almost never pl. participles; cf. IGT 10:4: ὁ δὲ ὄχλος ἰδὼν, προσεκύνησαν). παριστήκεισαν = (CG) παρειστήκεισαν: 3rd pl. pluperf. (= imperf.) act. indic. < παρίστημι.

15:5 μὴ, ἄπειρος: an example of *litotes*, a rhetorical device in which understatement is employed for rhetorical effect, via the use of double negatives, with the intention of emphasis. ἐστιν: Hock (134) notes that Weissengruber says that, "the indicative can be used in expressions of concern, if the concern is directed to something already happening." ἄπειρος: sc. Jesus' powers/temper.

15:6 ἵνα εἰδῇς: literally, *in order that you know*, i.e., *I want you to know*. ὡς: *as*.

15:7 ὡς + aor. indic = *when, after*. προσεγέλασεν: + dat. in LG; + acc. in CG.

Vocabulary

ἀδελφός, ὁ, *brother*

αἴρω, ἀρῶ, ἦρα, *take, take away, remove*

ἀξιόω, (contracted form, ἀξιῶ) (LG) *ask, request, beg*

ἄπειρος, -ον, *inexperienced (in), unacquainted (with), ignorant (of)*

αὐτός, -ή, -ό, (CG, pron. in gen., dat., acc.) *him, her, it, them*; (LG, pron. in all cases) *he, she, it, they*

διδασκαλεῖον, τό, *school*

διδασκαλία, ἡ, *teaching*

ἐπειδή, conj., *since, because, for; when, after*

ἑτοιμασία, ἡ, (LG) *readiness; preparation*

θαυμάζω, *be amazed, wonder at; admire*

λαλέω, (LG) *say, speak, tell*; (CG) *talk (aimlessly), chat, babble*

λογίζομαι, *think, suppose*

λοιπόν, adv., *from now on, henceforth; in addition*

μαθητής, οῦ, ὁ, *student*

μεστός, -ή, -όν, *full*

νήπιος, -α, -ον, *baby, infant, child*; (CG often =) *childish, silly*

ὀρθῶς, adv., *rightfully, correctly, properly*

ὅτι, conj., *that*

ὄχλος, ὁ, *crowd, multitude*

παραλάμβανω, παραλήψομαι, παρέλαβον, *take, receive, accept, take charge of*

παρίστημι, παραστήσω, (1ˢᵗ aor.) παρέστησα, *present, show*; (2ⁿᵈ aor.) παρέστην, (perf.) παρέστηκα, *stand by, be present*

προσγελάω, *look laughing at, smile upon*

σοφία, ἡ, *wisdom, insight, intelligence, knowledge*

συνέρχομαι, συνελεύσομαι, συνῆλθον, *come together, gather*

τοιοῦτος, τοιαύτη, τοιοῦτο, *such*

τρέχω, δραμοῦμαι, ἔδραμον, *run*

φθέγγομαι, *speak, utter*

φοβέομαι, *fear, be afraid of*

χάρις, -ιτος, ἡ, *grace, kindness, goodwill*; (LG) *a special manifestation of the divine presence, power,* or *glory*

ὡραιότης, -ητος, ἡ, (LG) *beauty; maturity*

ἐμαρτύρησας, διὰ σὲ κἀκεῖνος ὁ πληγωθεὶς ἰαθήσεται." καὶ

παραυτὰ ἰάθη ὁ ἕτερος καθηγητής. παρέλαβε δὲ Ἰωσὴφ τὸ

παιδίον καὶ ἀπῆλθεν εἰς τὸν οἶκον αὐτοῦ.

16. ἔπεμψε δὲ Ἰωσὴφ τὸν υἱὸν τὸν Ἰάκωβον τοῦ δῆσαι ξύλα

καὶ φέρειν εἰς τὸν οἶκον αὐτοῦ· ἠκολούθει δὲ καὶ τὸ παιδίον

Ἰησοῦς αὐτῷ. καὶ συλλέγοντος τοῦ Ἰάκωβου τὰ φρύγανα,

ἔχιδνα ἔδακε τὴν χεῖραν Ἰάκωβου. ² καὶ κατατεινομένου

αὐτοῦ καὶ ἀπολλυμένου προσήγγισεν ὁ Ἰησοῦς καὶ

κατεφύσησε τὸ δῆγμα· καὶ εὐθέως ἐπαύσατο ὁ πόνος, καὶ

τὸ θηρίον ἐρράγη, καὶ παραυτὰ ἔμεινεν ὁ Ἰάκωβος ὑγιής.

✕✕✕

15:7 διὰ σέ: *for your sake*; cf. 5.2. κἀκεῖνος: crasis for καὶ + ἐκεῖνος.
πληγωθείς: masc. nom. sing. aor. pass. part. < πληγόω; this refers to the
teacher who lost consciousness at 14:4 (apparently he was in a coma all this
time; though recall that according to CS 259 he had died).

16:1 τὸν Ἰάκωβον: James, the brother of Jesus (see Mark 6:3, Matthew
13:55). According to the NT, James became a follower of Jesus only after
the latter's resurrection, and quickly rose to a level of leadership in the early
Church (see Acts 15:13, 21:18-26; Galatians 2:9). τοῦ δῆσαι: the gen.
of the articular inf. can express purpose (the article should not be translated).
συλλέγοντος τοῦ Ἰάκωβου τὰ φρύγανα: gen. abs.

16:2 κατατεινομένου αὐτοῦ καὶ ἀπολλυμένου: gen. abs. ἐρράγη:
3rd sing. 2nd aor. pass. indic. < ῥήγνυμι; cf. Daniel 14:27, where Daniel feeds
the large serpent of the temple of the god Bel a boiled mixture of pitch, fat, and
hair: φαγὼν διερράγη ὁ δράκων (*upon eating it, the serpent burst apart*).
καὶ παραυτὰ ἔμεινεν ὁ Ἰάκωβος ὑγιής: the peculiar use of μένω
here may have engendered such later variations as: καὶ Ἰάκωβος ἐστάθη
(*and James stood up*; CS 259) and καὶ ἰάθη Ἰάκωβος (*and James was
healed*; CA 355).

Vocabulary

ἀκολουθέω, *follow, accompany*

ἀπέρχομαι, ἀπελεύσομαι, ἀπῆλθον, *go, go away, depart*

ἀπολλύμι, ἀπολέσω / ἀπολῶ, ἀπώλεσα, *destroy, kill; lose;* (mid.) *die; be lost, perish*

δάκνω, δήξομαι, ἔδακον, *bite*

δέω, *tie, bind*

δῆγμα, -ατος, τό, *bite, sting*

ἕτερος, -α, -ον, *other, another*

ἔχιδνα, -ης, ἡ, *snake, viper*

θηρίον, τό, (LG) *poisonous animal, reptile, snake;* (CG) *wild animal, beast*

Ἰάκωβος, ὁ, *James; Jacob*

ἰάομαι, *heal, cure; restore*

κατατείνω, *stretch, stretch out;* (pass.) *stretch on the ground; lay at full length*

καταφυσάω, (LG) *blow on*

μαρτυρέω, *bear witness, give evidence, testify; attest, affirm, speak well of*

μένω, *remain, stay;* (LG) *live; continue*

ξύλον, τό, *wood*

παραυτά, adv., *at once, immediately*

παραλάμβανω, παραλήψομαι, παρέλαβον, *take, receive, accept, take charge of*

παύω, *stop*

πέμπω, *send*

πληγόω (LG alternative form of πλήσσω), *strike*

πόνος, ὁ, *pain, suffering*

προσεγγίζω, *approach*

ῥήγνυμι (also ῥηγνύω and ῥήσσω), *break, break in pieces;* (pass.) *burst (apart)*

συλλέγω, *collect, gather*

ὑγιής, -ές, *sound, healthy; well, cured*

υἱός, ὁ, *son*

φρύγανον, τό, *dry wood, stick*

χείρ, χειρός, ἡ, *hand*

17. μετὰ δὲ ταῦτα ἐν τῇ γειτονίᾳ τοῦ Ἰωσὴφ νοσῶν τι νήπιον

ἀπέθανεν, καὶ ἔκλαιεν ἡ μήτηρ αὐτοῦ σφόδρα. ἤκουσε δὲ

ὁ Ἰησοῦς ὅτι πένθος μέγα καὶ θόρυβος γίνεται, καὶ ἔδραμε

σπουδαίως.

² καὶ εὑρὼν τὸ παιδίον νεκρόν, καὶ ἥψατο τοῦ στήθους

αὐτοῦ καὶ εἶπεν· "σοὶ λέγω, βρέφος, μὴ ἀποθάνῃς ἀλλὰ

ζῆσον, καὶ ἔστω μετὰ τῆς μητρός σου."

³ καὶ εὐθὺς ἀναβλέψας ἐγέλασεν. εἶπεν δὲ τῇ γυναικί·

"ἆρον τὸ παιδίον σου καὶ δὸς αὐτῷ μασθὸν καὶ μνημόνευέ

μου."

✕✕

17:1 γίνεται: verbs can agree in number with the nearest of two or more subjects.
17:2 καὶ ἥψατο: καὶ is superfluous here. "σοὶ λέγω,...σου.": Jesus' words
to the child are structurally similar to those he speaks to the dead man he brings
back to life at 18:2, and to the words he speaks in Mark's gospel to the paralytic
that he has healed (2:11): "σοὶ λέγω, ἔγειρε ἆρον τὸν κράβαττόν σου καὶ
ὕπαγε εἰς τὸν οἶκόν σου." ("I say to you, get up, take your cot and go to your
house."). Cf. also the accounts of Jesus bringing back from death a 12-year old
girl in the NT (Mark 5:41-2; Luke 8:54-55) and the widow's son at Nain (Luke
7:14). ἀποθάνῃς: 2nd sing. aor. act. subju. < ἀποθνήσκω; μή + 2nd-person
aor. subju. = a negative command equivalent to μή + impera. ζῆσον: 2nd
sing. aor. act. impera. < ζάω. ἔστω: 3rd sing. pres. impera. < εἰμί; in LG
(especially in the NT), 3rd-person imperatives are very often equivalent to
2nd-person imperatives.
17:3 ἀναβλέψας: grammatically this should be neut. to agree with its
understood subj., βρέφος/παιδίον; when the subj. is understood, as here, a
writer (especially in LG) may simply employ the masc. case. εἶπεν: sc. Jesus
as subj. ἆρον, δὸς, μνημόνευέ: note the change in aspect in the last of
the three imperatives.

Vocabulary

αἴρω, ἀρῶ, ἦρα, *take, take up*

ἀναβλέπω, *look up*

ἀποθνήσκω, ἀποθανοῦμαι, ἀπέθανον, *die*

ἅπτω, *light, ignite*; (mid. + gen.) *take hold of, touch*

βρέφος, -ους, τό, *baby, infant*

γειτονία, ἡ, *neighborhood*

γελάω, *laugh*

γυνή, -αικός, ἡ, *woman, wife*

δίδωμι, δώσω, ἔδωκα, *give*

εὐθύς, adv., *immediately, at once; straight, directly*; (LG) *then*

εὑρίσκω, εὑρήσω, ηὗρον / εὗρον, *find*

ζάω, (unattested hypothetical form) *live, be alive*

θόρυμος, ὁ, *confusion, disturbance*

κλαίω, *cry, weep, weep for*

μασθός, ὁ, (LG alternative form of μαστός) *breast*

μνημονεύω, *remember, keep in mind; make mention of*

νεκρός, ὁ, *corpse, dead body*

νήπιος, -α, -ον, *baby, infant, child*; (CG often =) *childish, silly*

νοσέω, *be sick*

ὅτι, conj., *that*

παίζω, *play*

πένθος, -ους, τό, *(public) mourning, sorrow, grief*

σπουδαίως, adv., *with haste, energetically*

στῆθος, -ους, τό, *chest, breast*

σφόδρα, adv., *very much, greatly*

⁴ καὶ ἰδὼν ὁ παρεστὼς ὄχλος ἐθαύμασεν, καὶ εἶπον·

"ἀληθῶς τὸ παιδίον τοῦτο ἢ θεὸς ἢ ἄγγελος θεοῦ ἐστιν,

ὅτι πᾶς λόγος αὐτοῦ ἔργον ἐστὶν ἕτοιμον." καὶ ἐξῆλθεν

ὁ Ἰησοῦς ἐκεῖθεν παίζων μετὰ καὶ ἑτέρων παιδίων.

18. μετὰ δὲ ἕτερον ἔτος οἰκοδομῆς γενομένης ἄνθρωπός

τις πεσὼν ἀπὸ τοῦ ὕψους ἀπέθανε. καὶ θορύβου μεγάλου,

ἵστατο ὁ Ἰησοῦς καὶ ἀπῆλθεν ἕως ἐκεῖ. ² καὶ ἰδών ἄνθρωπον

νεκρὸν κείμενον ἐπελάβετο τῆς χειρὸς αὐτοῦ καὶ εἶπεν·

"σοὶ λέγω, ἄνθρωπε, ἀνάστα, ποίει τὸ ἔργον σου." καὶ

εὐθέως ἀναστὰς προσεκύνησεν αὐτόν.

³ ἰδὼν δὲ ὁ ὄχλος ἐθαύμασεν καὶ εἶπεν· "τοῦτο τὸ παιδίον

οὐράνιόν ἐστιν· πολλὰς γὰρ ψυχὰς ἔσωσεν ἐκ θανάτου, καὶ

ἔχει σῶσαι ἕως πάσης τῆς ζωῆς αὐτοῦ."

×××

17:4 παρεστὼς: masc. nom. sing. perf. act. part. < παρίστημι. ἐθαύμασεν, εἶπον: either ἐθαύμασεν should be pl. or εἶπον should be sing.; cf. 15:4 and 18:3. ἢ θεὸς, ἢ ἄγγελος: cf. 7:11. ὅτι πᾶς λόγος αὐτοῦ ἔργον ἐστὶν ἕτοιμον: cf. 4:3. καὶ ἑτέρων: the καὶ is superfluous.

18:1 οἰκοδομῆς γενομένης: gen. abs.; CG would use the pres. part. (γιγνομένης) to express action that is *contemporaneous* (i.e., *while* a building was being constructed) with the main verbal ideas (πεσὼν, ἀπέθανε) of the sentence. θορύβου μεγάλου: gen. abs. (sc. ὄντος or γινομένου). ἵστατο: 3ʳᵈ sing. imperf. mid. indic. < ἵστημι; *stood up.*
18:2 ἀνάστα, ποίει: note the difference in aspect of these two imperatives.

56

Vocabulary

ἄγγελος, ὁ, *angel*; (CG) *messenger*

ἀληθῶς, *truly, in truth*

ἄνθρωπός, ὁ, *man, human being*

ἀνίστημι, ἀναστήσω, ἀνέστησα, *make X stand up, raise X*; (LG) *raise* (from the dead); (2nd aor.) ἀνέστην, *stand up, rise*

ἀπέρχομαι, ἀπελεύσομαι, ἀπῆλθον, *go, go away, depart*

ἐκεῖ, adv., *there, that place*

ἐκεῖθεν, adv., *from there*

ἐξέρχομαι, ἐξελεύσομαι, ἐξῆλθον, *go out, depart*

ἐπιλαμβάνω, ἐπιλήψομαι, ἐπέλαβον, *take*; (mid. + gen.) *take, take hold of*

ἔργον, τό, *work, deed*

ἕτερος, -α, -ον, *other, another*

ἕτοιμος, -η, -ον, *carried into effect, made good, already done*

ἔτος, -ους, τό, *year*

εὐθέως, adv., *immediately, at once*

ἔχω, ἕξω, ἔσχον, *have; hold*; (+ inf.) *can, be able, must; have* (sc. the power)

ἕως, conj., *until, as far as*; (LG, prep. + gen.) *as far as, throughout*

ζωή, ἡ, *life*

θάνατος, ὁ, *death*

θαυμάζω, *be amazed, wonder at; admire*

θόρυμος, ὁ, *confusion, disturbance*

ἵστημι, στήσω, ἔστησα, *make X stand; stop X; set X (up)*; (2nd aor.) ἔστην, (perf.) ἕστηκα, *stand*

κεῖμαι, κείσομαι, *lie*

μέγας, μεγάλη, μέγα, *large, great*

νεκρός, -ά, -όν, *dead, lifeless*

οἰκοδομή, ἡ, (LG) *building, structure, house*

οὐράνιος, -ον, *heavenly, from heaven*

ὄχλος, ὁ, *crowd, multitude*

παρίστημι, παραστήσω, (1st aor.) παρέστησα, *present, show*; (2nd aor.) παρέστην, (perf.) παρέστηκα, *stand by, be present*

πίπτω, πεσοῦμαι, ἔπεσον, *fall*

προσκυνέω, *worship, fall down and worship*

σώζω, *save, rescue, deliver; cure, make well*

ὕψος, -ους, τό, *height*

χείρ, χειρός, ἡ, *hand*

ψυχή, ἡ, *life, life-force, soul, spirit; person, human being*

19. ὄντος δὲ αὐτοῦ δωδεκαετοῦς ἐπορεύοντο οἱ γονεῖς

αὐτοῦ κατὰ τὸ ἔθος εἰς Ἰερουσαλὴμ εἰς τὴν ἑορτὴν τοῦ

πάσχα μετὰ τῆς συνοδίας αὐτῶν, ² καὶ μετὰ τὸ πάσχα

ὑπέστρεφον εἰς τὸν οἶκον αὐτῶν. καὶ ἐν τῷ ὑποστρέφειν

αὐτοὺς ἀνῆλθε τὸ παιδίον Ἰησοῦς εἰς Ἰερουσαλὴμ·

οἱ δὲ γονεῖς αὐτοῦ ἐνόμισαν αὐτὸν ἐν τῇ συνοδίᾳ εἶναι.

³ ὁδευσάντων δὲ ὁδὸν ἡμέρας μιᾶς, ἐζήτουν αὐτὸν ἐν τοῖς

συγγενέσιν αὐτῶν, καὶ μὴ εὑρόντες αὐτὸν ἐλυπήθησαν,

καὶ ὑπέστρεψαν πάλιν εἰς τὴν πόλιν ζητοῦντες αὐτόν.

⁴ καὶ μετὰ τρίτην ἡμέραν εὗρον αὐτὸν ἐν τῷ ἱερῷ

καθεζόμενον ἐν μέσῳ τῶν διδασκάλων καὶ ἀκούοντα τοῦ

νόμου καὶ ἐρωτῶντα αὐτούς. ⁵ προσεῖχον δὲ πάντες καὶ

✕✕✕

19:1 ὄντος δὲ αὐτοῦ δωδεκαετοῦς: gen. abs. **πάσχα**: this festival, celebrated at the beginning of the Jewish year on the fourteenth day of the month of Nisan (March/April), commemorates the Exodus of the Hebrews from Egypt. Since Jerusalem was *c.* eighty miles from Jesus' hometown of Nazareth, the trip would take at least three days.   From here to the end of IGT the narrative closely follows that of Luke 2:41-51 (see **Appendix 1**).

19:2 ἐν τῷ ὑποστρέφειν αὐτούς: ἐν τῷ + inf. is a type of articular inf. most often used to express contemporaneous time, i.e., *while they were returning*.

19:3 ὁδευσάντων δὲ ὁδὸν ἡμέρας μιᾶς: gen. abs. (sc. αὐτῶν); in CG the subj. of a gen. abs. clause is almost never grammatically linked to the main clause of the sentence. **ἐλυπήθησαν**: 3rd pl. aor. pass. indic. < λυπέω. **ζητοῦντες**: CG would use ὡς + the fut. part. (or the fut. part. without ὡς) to express purpose, i.e., *to look for him*.

19:5 προσεῖχον: sc. αὐτόν, i.e., Jesus, as direct object.

Vocabulary

ἀνέρχομαι, ἀνελεύσομαι, ἀνεξῆλθον, *go up, go back*

διδάσκαλος, ὁ, *teacher*

δωδεκαετής, -ές, *twelve years old*

ἔθος, -ους, τό, *custom, habit*

εἷς, μία, ἕν, *one*

ἑορτή, ἡ, *festival, feast*

ἐρωτάω, *ask (a question)*

εὑρίσκω, εὑρήσω, ηὗρον / εὗρον, *find*

ζητέω, *seek, look for*

ἡμέρα, ἡ, *day*

ἱερόν, τό, *temple, temple precinct*

Ἰερουσαλήμ, (indecl.) *Jerusalem*

καθέζομαι, *sit, sit down*

λυπέω, *vex, cause grief or pain to* X, *injure*; (pass.) *be sad, sorrowful or distressed; grieve*

μέσος, -η, -ον, *middle, in the middle*

νομίζω, *think, suppose, assume*

νόμος, ὁ, (LG) *law* (i.e., the Jewish sacred tradition, especially that found in the Old Testament); (CG) *custom, usage, law; pasture; province, district*

ὁδεύω, *go, travel, journey*

ὁδός, ὁδοῦ, ἡ, *road, way, journey*

πάλιν, adv., *back*

πάσχα, τό, (indecl.) *Passover*

πορεύομαι, *go, walk, journey*

προσέχω, προσέξω, προσέσχον, *pay close attention to*

πῶς, adv., *how?, in what manner or way?*

συγγενής, -οῦς, ὁ, *relative*

συνοδία, ἡ, *group of travelers*

τρίτος, -η, -ον, *third*

ὑποστρέφω, *return, turn back*

ἐθαύμαζον, πῶς παιδίον ὑπάρχων ἀποστοματίζει τοὺς

πρεσβυτέρους καὶ διδασκάλους τοῦ λαοῦ, ἐπιλύων τὰ

κεφάλαια τοῦ νόμου καὶ τὰς παραβολὰς τῶν προφητῶν.

⁶ προσελθοῦσα δὲ ἡ μήτηρ αὐτοῦ Μαρία εἶπεν αὐτῷ·

"ἵνα τί τοῦτο ἐποίησας ἡμῖν, τέκνον; ἰδοὺ ὀδυνώμενοι

ἐζητοῦμέν σε."

⁷ καὶ εἶπεν αὐτοῖς ὁ Ἰησοῦς· "τί με ζητεῖτε; οὐκ οἴδατε

ὅτι ἐν τοῖς τοῦ πατρός μου δεῖ εἶναί με;"

✳✳

19.5 ἀποστοματίζει: this is the reading of CA 355, Greek-Slav, and CS 259 (which uses the imperf.); Tischendorf A has ἀποστομίζει (*put to silence*). τοῦ νόμου καὶ...τῶν προφητῶν: to Jews and Christians ὁ νόμος is God's revelation through Moses to Israel as revealed in the first five books of the Hebrew Scriptures/Old Testament (i.e., Genesis, Exodus, Leviticus, Numbers, and Deuteronomy). οἱ προφῆται refers either to all the remaining books in the Hebrew Scriptures/Old Testament (i.e., the historical books, the wisdom books, and the major and minor prophets; in which case the phrase νόμος καὶ προφῆται is thus simply a circumlocution for the totality of the Hebrew Scriptures/Old Testament) or specifically to the major and minor prophetical works (i.e., Isaiah, Jeremiah, etc.).

19:6 ἵνα τί = ἵνα τί γένηται: literally, *in order that what might happen?*, i.e., *for what purpose* or *reason?, why?*

19:7 οἴδατε ὅτι ἐν τοῖς τοῦ πατρός μου δεῖ εἶναί με; = οἴδατε ὅτι δεῖ με εἶναί ἐν τοῖς τοῦ πατρός μου; ἐν τοῖς τοῦ πατρός μου: an elliptical, somewhat enigmatic phrase. As Hock notes (143), "The ambiguity arises because in the phrase εἶναί ἐν τοῖς τοῦ πατρός μου there is no noun for the article τοῖς. One must be supplied, and most scholars have proposed "house,"...on the grounds that context requires a noun answering the question where. Some scholars, however, prefer to supply "affairs," so that the phrase would mean something like "concerned with my father's business." Recently, scholars are preferring to keep the ambiguity and supply both nouns." Ehrman/Pleše also offer a third possibility: "with those who are my Father's," i.e., the scribes/scholars and Pharisees (see 19:8) debating the meaning of the Hebrew Scriptures in the Temple.

Vocabulary

ἀποστοματίζω, (LG) *attack with questions, question sharply*; (CG) *dictate; recite, repeat by heart*

δεῖ, (impersonal) *it is necessary, must; should, ought; it is proper*

διδάσκαλος, ὁ, *teacher*

ἐπιλύω, (LG) *explain; settle (a dispute)*; (CG) *loose, untie, set free*

ζητέω, *seek, look for*

ἰδού, adv., *look!*

κεφάλαιον, τό, *main point*

λαός, ὁ, *people*

Μαρία, ἡ, *Mary*

μήτηρ, μητρός, ἡ, *mother*

νόμος, ὁ, (LG) *law* (i.e., the Jewish sacred tradition, especially that found in the Old Testament); (CG) *custom, usage, law; pasture; province, district*

ὀδυνάομαι, *be in great pain; be deeply distressed* or *worried*

οὔτε, conj., *and not, not, nor*

παραβολή, ἡ, (LG) *parable, proverb*; (CG) *comparison, illustration, analogy*

ποτέ, (enclitic particle) *ever*

πρεσβύτερος, ὁ, *elder* (of the Jewish religious leaders)

προσέρχομαι, προσελεύσομαι, προσεξῆλθον, *go* or *come forward, approach*

προφήτης, -ου, ὁ, *prophet*; (LG) οἱ προφῆται = *prophetic books of the Hebrew Scriptures/Old Testament*

τέκνον, τό, *child*; (in the voc. for familiar address) *my child.*

ὑπάρχω (= εἰμί), *be*

⁸ οἱ δὲ γραμματεῖς καὶ οἱ Φαρισαῖοι εἶπον· "σὺ εἶ μήτηρ τοῦ παιδίου τούτου;"

⁹ ἡ δὲ εἶπεν· "ἐγώ εἰμι."

¹⁰ καὶ εἶπον αὐτῇ· "μακαρία σὺ εἶ ἐν γυναιξίν, ὅτι ηὐλόγησεν ὁ θεὸς τὸν καρπὸν τῆς κοιλίας σου· τοιαύτην γὰρ δόξαν καὶ τοιαύτην ἀρετὴν καὶ σοφίαν οὔτε ἠκούσαμέν ποτε."

¹¹ ἀναστὰς δὲ Ἰησοῦς ἠκολούθησεν τῇ μητρὶ αὐτοῦ, καὶ ἦν ὑποτασσόμενος τοῖς γονεῦσιν αὐτοῦ. ἡ δὲ μήτηρ αὐτοῦ διετήρει πάντα τὰ γενόμενα. ¹² ὁ δε Ἰησοῦς προέκοπτε σοφίᾳ καὶ ἡλικίᾳ καὶ χάριτι.

¹³ αὐτῷ ἡ δόξα εἰς τοὺς αἰῶνας τῶν αἰώνων, ἀμήν.

✗✗

19:8 γραμματεῖς: these were scribes or scholars, i.e., men who were experts in Jewish religious law. In the NT, scribes are shown arguing with Jesus over legal matters, dietary laws, purity laws, interpretation of scripture, and Sabbath observance.   Φαρισαῖοι: the Pharisees were a movement that figured prominently in the political, social, and religious debates that took place in Palestine from *c*. 140 BCE to 70 CE. After the Roman destruction of the Second Temple in 70 CE, their beliefs became the foundation for Rabbinic Judaism. In the NT, Jesus is often depicted in conflict with the Pharisees (see note to ἐβεβήλωσεν τὸ σάββατον at 2:4).
19:10 οὔτε, ποτε = οὐδέποτε (*never*).
19:11 ἦν ὑποτασσόμενος: cf. Joseph's words at 6:3. διετήρει πάντα τὰ γενόμενα: cf. Mary's actions at 11:4.
19:13 αὐτῷ: i.e., Jesus. ἡ δόξα: sc. ἔστω (the 3ʳᵈ sing. impera. of εἰμί). εἰς τοὺς αἰῶνας τῶν αἰώνων: literally, *into the ages of the ages*, i.e., *forever and ever, for all eternity*.

Vocabulary

αἰών, -ῶνος, ὁ, *age, generation, epoch, era*

ἀκολουθέω, *follow, accompany*

ἀμήν, (LG transliterated from Hebrew) *amen; so be it; truly, indeed.*

ἀνίστημι, ἀναστήσω, ἀνέστησα, *make X stand up, raise X;* (LG) *raise* (from the dead); (2nd aor.) ἀνέστην, *stand up, rise*

ἀρετή, ἡ, *moral excellence, goodness, virtue*

γονεύς, γονέως, ὁ, *father;* (pl.) *parents*

γραμματεύς, γραμματέως, ὁ, *scribe, expert in the Jewish law; clerk, scholar*

γυνή, -αικός, ἡ, *woman, wife*

διετηρέω, *keep, keep faithfully*

δόξα, ἡ, *glory*

εὐλογέω, (LG) *bless;* (CG) *speak well of, praise, honor*

ἡλικία, ἡ, *age*

καρπός, ὁ, *fruit*

κοιλία, ἡ, *womb; stomach, belly*

μακάριος, -α, -ον, *blessed, fortunate, happy*

μήτηρ, μητρός, ἡ, *mother*

προκόπτω, *advance, progress, grow*

σοφία, ἡ, *wisdom, insight, intelligence, knowledge*

ὑποτάσσω, *rule, control, subordinate;* (pass.) *be obedient to, obey*

Φαρισαῖος, ὁ, *Pharisee*

χάρις, -ιτος, ἡ, *grace, kindness, goodwill;* (LG) *a special manifestation of the divine presence, power,* or *glory*

Appendix 1:

Luke 2:41-52 and IGT 19

A comparative analysis of IGT's concluding chapter (19), at least in terms of the text that is printed in this edition (which mostly follows Tischendorf A), with the text on which it is based, Luke 2:41-52 (UBS 4th ed., revised), reveals two significant modifications made by IGT to Luke's narrative: (1) IGT places greater emphasis on the remarkable intellectual talents of a 12-year old child as recognized by adult experts (19:5); (2) IGT displays greater interest in the role of Jesus' parents (cf. 19:3 and note ad loc.), in particular that of his mother, who is singled out as worthy of special praise (19:8-10).[22]

Also of interest when comparing these two narratives are their respective prose styles. Luke is generally credited with belonging to the group of texts in the NT classified as "Literary Koine," whereas all of the Greek manuscripts of IGT possess grammatical and syntactic features common to texts such as Mark's gospel and Revelation, works that are classified as belonging to a lower literary level of Koine, sometimes labeled "Semitic/Vulgar."[23]

However, a comparative analysis of the grammar and syntax of Luke 2:41-52 with IGT 19 seems to show that such categories are sometimes too simplistic.

---

[22] For a detailed exploration of the relationship of IGT as a supplement to the Gospel of Luke, see T. Chartrand-Burke, "Completing the Gospel: *The Infancy Gospel of Thomas* as a Supplement to the Gospel of Luke," in *The Reception and Interpretation of the Bible in Late Antiquity: Proceedings of the Montreal Colloquium in Honour of Charles Kannengieser, 11-13 October, 2006*, edited by L. DiTommaso and L. Turescu (Brill: 2008), 101-119. Aasgaard, *The Childhood of Jesus*, 115-118 provides a succinct comparison of CS 259's text of 19 (ch. 17 in that manuscript) to Luke 2:41-52.

[23] For the classification of these texts, see D. Wallace, *Greek Grammar Beyond the Basics* (Grand Rapids: Zondervan, 1996), 17-30.

The reasons for this are not hard to find. IGT, after all, is made up of various linguistic and stylistic layers that developed over the course of its oral-literary evolution lasting more than a millennium. In addition, it is important to remember an interrelated fact about IGT that contributed significantly to the evolution of its text: it was never a canonical work, and so there was never any authority invested in policing its changes over time. Indeed, both the various Greek and versional textual families clearly evince a narrative that was shaped to satisfy individual communities' slightly different ideas concerning the central figure in their religion.[24]

For these reasons, then, it should not come as much of a surprise to discover that IGT's prose, at least in terms of that found in Tischendorf A, is not necessarily always a simplified or more "crude" version of Luke's more sophisticated style. Consider, for example, the following:

In Luke 2:44,

νομίσαντες δὲ αὐτὸν εἶναι ἐν τῇ συνοδίᾳ ἦλθον ἡμέρας ὁδὸν καὶ ἀνεζήτουν αὐτὸν ἐν τοῖς συγγενεῦσιν καὶ τοῖς γνωστοῖς, . . .

(*But having thought that he was in their group of travelers, they went a day's journey, and they began to search for him among their relatives and acquaintances,...*)[25]

the two clauses employing indicative verbs are rather clumsily – at least in terms of sense – joined by καί. In fact, the use of καί in this instance is typical of "Semitic/Vulgar" Koine and its reliance on paratactic syntax.

---

[24] See **Appendix 4** for a listing of 16 additional episodes from Jesus' childhood found in non-Greek versions of IGT.

[25] Two of the most widely-used contemporary English translations of the NT eliminate the awkwardness of Luke' Greek:

NIV: *Thinking he was in their company, they traveled on for a day. Then they began looking for him among their relatives and friends.*

NRSV: *Assuming that he was in the group of travelers, they went a day's journey. Then they started to look for him among their relatives and friends.*

Compare the Lukan version with IGT 19:2-3 (Tischendorf A),

οἱ δὲ γονεῖς αὐτοῦ ἐνόμισαν αὐτὸν ἐν τῇ συνοδίᾳ εἶναι.
ὁδευσάντων δὲ ὁδὸν ἡμέρας μιᾶς, ἐζήτουν αὐτὸν ἐν
τοῖς συγγενέσιν αὐτῶν, . . .

(*But his parents thought that he was in their group of travelers.
But after they had journeyed one day's journey, they began to
look for him among their relatives,...*)

which employs a genitive absolute to eliminate the awkward
conjunction of the Lukan clauses.[26]

Codex Sabaiticus 259's text of IGT, however, which may preserve
an earlier version of that work's ending,[27] is closer to Luke's prose:

. . . νομίσαντες εἶναι αὐτὸν ἐν τῇ συνοδίᾳ. ἦλθαν
ἡμέρας ὁδὸν καὶ ἐζήτουν αὐτὸν ἐν τοῖς συγγενεῦσιν
καὶ ἐν τοῖς γνωστοῖς αὐτῶν, . . .

([*And his parents did not know* (sc. it)], *having thought that he
was in their group of travelers. They went a day's journey and
they began to look for him among their relatives and among
their acquaintances,...*).

Because Luke 2:41-52 and IGT 19 cover the same episode, and
because the latter appears to be an intentional retelling of the former
(though both may have originated in a shared oral tradition), these
two texts afford an excellent opportunity for students of Ancient
Greek to develop their skills at discerning the particular qualities of
prose style that differentiate one text from another (and in the case of
IGT, one manuscript from another).

---

[26] IGT's use of the gen. abs. here does contravene CG grammatical norms by
having the subject of the gen. abs. clause be grammatically linked to the rest of the
sentence. In LG, however, the gen. abs. often functions in this way. Note too the
rhetorical effect created by the cognates: ὁδευσάντων, ὁδὸν.

[27] Or, what is possible but less likely, the text at this point has undergone
harmonization; i.e., a scribe has intentionally rewritten part of the text so that it
more closely matches Luke's account.

Luke 2:41-45

⁴¹ καὶ ἐπορεύοντο οἱ γονεῖς αὐτοῦ κατ᾽ ἔτος εἰς Ἰερουσαλὴμ τῇ ἑορτῇ τοῦ πάσχα. ⁴² καὶ ὅτε ἐγένετο ἐτῶν δώδεκα, ἀναβαινόντων αὐτῶν κατὰ τὸ ἔθος τῆς ἑορτῆς ⁴³ καὶ τελειωσάντων τὰς ἡμέρας, ἐν τῷ ὑποστρέφειν αὐτοὺς ὑπέμεινεν Ἰησοῦς ὁ παῖς ἐν Ἰερουσαλήμ, καὶ οὐκ ἔγνωσαν οἱ γονεῖς αὐτοῦ. ⁴⁴ νομίσαντες δὲ αὐτὸν εἶναι ἐν τῇ συνοδίᾳ ἦλθον ἡμέρας ὁδὸν καὶ ἀνεζήτουν αὐτὸν ἐν τοῖς συγγενεῦσιν καὶ τοῖς γνωστοῖς, ⁴⁵ καὶ μὴ εὑρόντες ὑπέστρεψαν εἰς Ἰερουσαλὴμ ἀναζητοῦντες αὐτόν.

Infancy Gospel of Thomas 19:1-3

19. ὄντος δὲ αὐτοῦ δωδεκαετοῦς ἐπορεύοντο οἱ γονεῖς αὐτοῦ κατὰ τὸ ἔθος εἰς Ἰερουσαλὴμ εἰς τὴν ἑορτὴν τοῦ πάσχα μετὰ τῆς συνοδίας αὐτῶν, ² καὶ μετὰ τὸ πάσχα ὑπέστρεφον εἰς τὸν οἶκον αὐτῶν. καὶ ἐν τῷ ὑποστρέφειν αὐτοὺς ἀνῆλθε τὸ παιδίον Ἰησοῦς εἰς Ἰερουσαλήμ· οἱ δὲ γονεῖς αὐτοῦ ἐνόμισαν αὐτὸν ἐν τῇ συνοδίᾳ εἶναι. ³ ὁδευσάντων δὲ ὁδὸν ἡμέρας μιᾶς, ἐζήτουν αὐτὸν ἐν τοῖς συγγενέσιν αὐτῶν, καὶ μὴ εὑρόντες αὐτὸν ἐλυπήθησαν, καὶ ὑπέστρεψαν πάλιν εἰς τὴν πόλιν ζητοῦντες αὐτόν.

✕✕

IGT 19:2: note the substitution of ἀνῆλθε for ὑπέμεινεν (Luke 2:43), giving both greater plausibility as to why Jesus' parents did not look for him until after a day had passed and also showing them as more concerned about their son: they did not simply assume he had set out with them homeward; he actually did do so.
IGT 19:3: note the addition of ἐλυπήθησαν, which provides an emotional response on the part of the parents lacking in the Lukan narrative at this point.

Vocabulary

ἀναβαίνω, *go up,*

ἀναζήτεω, *search after, look for*

ἀνέρχομαι, ἀνελεύσομαι, ἀνεξῆλθον, *go up, go back*

ἀποστοματίζω, (LG) *attack with questions, question sharply*; (CG) *dictate; recite, repeat by heart*

γι(γ)νώσκω, γνώσομαι, ἔγνων, *know*

γνωστός, -ή, -όν, *known; acquaintance, friend*

δωδεκαετής, -ές, *twelve years old*

ἔθος, -ους, τό, *custom, habit*

εἷς, μία, ἔν, *one*

ἑορτή, ἡ, *festival, feast*

ἔτος, -ους, τό, *year*

εὑρίσκω, εὑρήσω, ηὗρον / εὗρον, *find*

ζητέω, *seek, look for*

ἡμέρα, -ας, ἡ, *day*

Ἰερουσαλὴμ, ἡ, (indecl.) *Jerusalem*

κεφάλαιον, τό, *main point*

λαός, ὁ, *people*

λυπέω, *vex, cause grief or pain to* X, *injure*; (pass.) *be sad, sorrowful or distressed; grieve*

νομίζω, *think, suppose, assume*

νόμος, ὁ, (LG) *law* (i.e., the Jewish sacred tradition, especially that found in the Old Testament); (CG) *custom, usage, law; pasture; province, district*

ὁδεύω, *go, travel, journey*

ὁδός, ὁδοῦ, ἡ, *road, way, journey*

πάλιν, adv., *back*

πάσχα, τό, (indecl.) *Passover*

πορεύομαι, *go, walk, journey*

συγγενής, -οῦς, ὁ, *relative*

συνοδία, ἡ, *group of travelers*

τελειόω, *complete, finish, accomplish*

ὑπομένω, *remain, stay behind*

ὑποστρέφω, *return, turn back*

Luke 2:46-48

⁴⁶ καὶ ἐγένετο μετὰ ἡμέρας τρεῖς εὗρον αὐτὸν ἐν τῷ ἱερῷ καθεζόμενον ἐν μέσῳ τῶν διδασκάλων καὶ ἀκούοντα αὐτῶν καὶ ἐπερωτῶντα αὐτούς· ⁴⁷ ἐξίσταντο δὲ πάντες οἱ ἀκούοντες αὐτοῦ ἐπὶ τῇ συνέσει καὶ ταῖς ἀποκρίσεσιν αὐτοῦ. ⁴⁸ καὶ ἰδόντες αὐτὸν ἐξεπλάγησαν, καὶ εἶπεν πρὸς αὐτὸν ἡ μήτηρ αὐτοῦ· "τέκνον, τί ἐποίησας ἡμῖν οὕτως; ἰδοὺ ὁ πατήρ σου κἀγὼ ὀδυνώμενοι ἐζητοῦμέν σε."

Infancy Gospel of Thomas 19:4-7

⁴ καὶ μετὰ τρίτην ἡμέραν εὗρον αὐτὸν ἐν τῷ ἱερῷ καθεζόμενον ἐν μέσῳ τῶν διδασκάλων καὶ ἀκούοντα τοῦ νόμου καὶ ἐρωτῶντα αὐτούς. ⁵ προσεῖχον δὲ πάντες καὶ ἐθαύμαζον, πῶς παιδίον ὑπάρχων ἀποστοματίζει τοὺς πρεσβυτέρους καὶ διδασκάλους τοῦ λαοῦ, ἐπιλύων τὰ κεφάλαια τοῦ νόμου καὶ τὰς παραβολὰς τῶν προφητῶν. ⁶ προσελθοῦσα δὲ ἡ μήτηρ αὐτοῦ Μαρία εἶπεν αὐτῷ· "ἵνα τί τοῦτο ἐποίησας ἡμῖν, τέκνον; ἰδοὺ ὀδυνώμενοι ἐζητοῦμέν σε."

✗✗

IGT 19:5: as Hock notes (141), "This verse represents a considerable expansion of its Lukan counterpart (see Luke 2:47). In particular, the paradox of a child teaching his elders is made explicit....as is the sort of intelligent answers he gave."

IGT 19:6: ἵνα τί τοῦτο ἐποίησας ἡμῖν, τέκνον;: the text of IGT employed here (Tischendorf A), with its transformation of Luke's adv. into a demonstrative adj. (which is used as the direct object of ἐποίησας), seems to be ironing out some of the perceived awkwardness of the Lukan text. CS 259 keeps the Lukan wording minus the adv. ὀδυνώμενοι ἐζητοῦμέν: CS 259 adds λυπούμενοι (*being distressed*) after ὀδυνώμενοι.

Vocabulary

ἀπόκρισις, -εως, ἡ, *answer, reply*

διδάσκαλος, ὁ, *teacher*

ἐκπλήσσομαι, (2nd aor.) ἐξεπλάγην, *be amazed*

ἐξίστημι, *be amazed* or *surprised* at; *be out of one's mind* (ἐξίσταντο is 3rd pl. imperf. mid. indic.; the mid. has the same meaning as the act.)

ἐπερωτάω, *ask (a question), ask for*

ἐπιλύω, (LG) *explain; settle (a dispute);* (CG) *loose, untie, set free*

ἐρωτάω, *ask (a question)*

εὑρίσκω, εὑρήσω, ηὗρον / εὗρον, *find*

ἡμέρα, -ας, ἡ, *day*

ἰδού, adv., *look!*

ἱερόν, τό, *temple, temple precinct*

καθέζομαι, *sit, sit down*

ζητέω, *seek, look for*

Μαρία, ἡ, *Mary*

μέσος, -η, -ον, *middle, in the middle*

μήτηρ, μητρός, ἡ, *mother*

νόμος, ὁ, (LG) *law* (i.e., the Jewish sacred tradition, especially that found in the Old Testament); (CG) *custom, usage, law; pasture; province, district*

ὀδυνάομαι, *be in great pain; be deeply distressed* or *worried*

οὔτε, conj., *and not, not, nor*

οὕτως, adv., *in this way, thus, so, like this*

παραβολή, ἡ, (LG) *parable, proverb;* (CG) *comparison, illustration, analogy*

ποτέ, (enclitic particle) *ever*

πρεσβύτερος, ὁ, *elder* (of the Jewish religious leaders)

προσέρχομαι, προσελεύσομαι, προσῆλθον, *go* or *come forward, approach*

προσέχω, προσέξω, προσέσχον, *pay close attention to*

προφήτης, ου, ὁ, *prophet;* (LG) προφῆται = *prophetic books of the Hebrew Scriptures/Old Testament*

πῶς, adv., *how?, in what manner* or *way?*

σύνεσις, -εως, ἡ, *understanding, power of comprehension, insight, intelligence*

τρεῖς, τρία, *three*

τρίτος, -η, -ον, *third*

Luke 2:49-52

⁴⁹ καὶ εἶπεν πρὸς αὐτούς· "τί ὅτι ἐζητεῖτέ με; οὐκ ἤδειτε ὅτι ἐν τοῖς τοῦ πατρός μου δεῖ εἶναί με; ⁵⁰ καὶ αὐτοὶ οὐ συνῆκαν τὸ ῥῆμα ὃ ἐλάλησεν αὐτοῖς. ⁵¹ καὶ κατέβη μετ' αὐτῶν καὶ ἦλθεν εἰς Ναζαρὲθ καὶ ἦν ὑποτασσόμενος αὐτοῖς. καὶ ἡ μήτηρ αὐτοῦ διετήρει πάντα τὰ ῥήματα ἐν τῇ καρδίᾳ αὐτῆς. ⁵² καὶ Ἰησοῦς προέκοπτεν [ἐν τῇ] σοφίᾳ καὶ ἡλικίᾳ καὶ χάριτι παρὰ θεῷ καὶ ἀνθρώποις.

Infancy Gospel of Thomas 19:7-13

⁷ καὶ εἶπεν αὐτοῖς ὁ Ἰησοῦς· "τί με ζητεῖτε; οὐκ οἴδατε ὅτι ἐν τοῖς τοῦ πατρός μου δεῖ εἶναί με;" ⁸ οἱ δὲ γραμματεῖς καὶ οἱ Φαρισαῖοι εἶπον· "σὺ εἶ μήτηρ τοῦ παιδίου τούτου;" ⁹ ἡ δὲ εἶπεν· "ἐγώ εἰμι." ¹⁰ καὶ εἶπον αὐτῇ· "μακαρία σὺ εἶ ἐν γυναιξίν, ὅτι ηὐλόγησεν ὁ θεὸς τὸν καρπὸν τῆς κοιλίας σου· τοιαύτην γὰρ δόξαν καὶ τοιαύτην ἀρετὴν καὶ σοφίαν οὔτε ἠκούσαμέν ποτε." ¹¹ ἀναστὰς δὲ Ἰησοῦς ἠκολούθησεν τῇ μητρὶ αὐτοῦ, καὶ ἦν ὑποτασσόμενος τοῖς γονεῦσιν αὐτοῦ. ἡ δὲ μήτηρ αὐτοῦ διετήρει πάντα τὰ γενόμενα. ¹² ὁ δε Ἰησοῦς προέκοπτε σοφίᾳ καὶ ἡλικίᾳ καὶ χάριτι. ¹³ αὐτῷ ἡ δόξα εἰς τοὺς αἰῶνας τῶν αἰώνων, ἀμήν.

✕✕

IGT 19:8-10: the account in Luke has no parallel to these verses. Hock notes (143) that "these verses replace v. 50 in Luke..., an omission which removes a negative characterization of Joseph and Mary. In contrast, at least Mary becomes the subject of an admiring beatitude (v. 10)."
IGT 19:13: IGT has a concluding doxology; Luke's story is just beginning.

Vocabulary

αἰών, -ῶνος, ὁ, *age, generation, epoch, era*

ἀκολουθέω, *follow, accompany*

ἀμήν, (LG transliterated from Hebrew) *amen; so be it; truly, indeed.*

ἀνίστημι, ἀναστήσω, ἀνέστησα, *make X stand up, raise X;* (LG) *raise* (*from the dead*); (2nd aor.) ἀνέστην, *stand up, rise*

ἀρετή, ἡ, *moral excellence, goodness, virtue*

γονεύς, γονέως, ὁ, *father;* (pl.) *parents*

γραμματεύς, γραμματέως, ὁ, *scribe, expert in the Jewish law; clerk, scholar*

γυνή, -αικός, ἡ, *woman, wife*

δεῖ, (impersonal) *it is necessary, must; should, ought; it is proper*

διετηρέω, *keep, keep faithfully*

δόξα, ἡ, *glory*

εὐλογέω, (LG) *bless;* (CG) *speak well of, praise, honor*

ζητέω, *seek, look for*

ἡλικία, ἡ, *age*

καρπός, ὁ, *fruit*

καταβαίνω, καταβήσομαι, κατέβη, *come* or *go down*

κοιλία, ἡ, *womb; stomach, belly*

μακάριος, -α, -ον, *blessed, fortunate, happy*

μήτηρ, μητρός, ἡ, *mother*

προκόπτω, *advance, progress, grow*

ῥῆμα, -τος, τό, *what is said, word, saying*

σοφία, ἡ, *wisdom, insight, intelligence, knowledge*

συνίημι, συνήσω, συνῆκαν, *understand, comprehend*

ὑποτάσσω, *rule, control, subordinate;* (pass.) *be obedient to, obey*

Φαρισαῖος, ὁ, *Pharisee*

χάρις, -ιτος, ἡ, *grace, kindness, goodwill;* (LG) *a special manifestation of the divine presence, power,* or *glory*

Appendix 2:

Illustration of Jesus Going to School (IGT 6:14)

The illustration below is from a 15th-century Latin manuscript in the Ambrosian Library (Milan; L 58 sup.) that contains the Gospel of Pseudo-Matthew (a redaction of the Infancy Gospel of James and IGT). The image, from left to right, depicts Joseph, Jesus (both with haloes) and Zacchaeus outside a school house. Jesus holds in his left hand a hornbook with a stylus dangling from its handle.[28] The classroom is packed with unruly students – a detail not explicitly mentioned in IGT's account. At least two hornbooks are on the ground (one inside and one outside the school).

---

[28] Hornbooks were first employed in the late medieval/early renaissance period to teach children how to read. On the hornbook, which consisted of a wooden frame with a handle, a vellum leaf (later a sheet of paper) containing the alphabet was covered with a sheet of transparent horn and fixed to the frame. The hornbook's analogue in the schools of the ancient world was the diptych: two pieces of wood tied together so that they could open and shut, with each piece having a shallow recess that was filled with wax. A stylus was then used to write on the wax surface.

Appendix 3:

Jesus' Alpha Lesson

As noted above in the commentary, Jesus' alpha lesson (6:22-23) is the most perplexing section of IGT since it is difficult to figure out what specific information the precocious young child is trying to impart about the first letter.

Aasgaard's interpretation of the passage (*The Childhood of Jesus*, 145-146), based on the slightly different reading of *Codex Sabaiticus 259*,[29] might offer a possible solution to understanding the nature and function of this passage, and so is quoted in full:

> "In my view, Jesus' exegesis of the alpha should be interpreted on the basis of such pedagogical strategies and experiences—this is far more likely than attempts at extracting gnostic or some esoteric meaning out of the passage. Parts of Jesus' exposition clearly refer to the form of the letter alpha, either written as the uncial A ("sharp lines," "a middle stroke," "sharpening," "joining," "equally-measured") or as cursive α ("dancing," "intersecting"). Other parts seem to play on numbers and words ("three-marked, double-edged," "same-formed, same-placed, same-kinded"), with some words being virtually unintelligible. Some terms may also refer to diacritical signs, such as dots and ligatures ("creeping out, drawing back, elevated").

---

[29] Surprisingly, all Greek versions that contain this passage are remarkably similar. This is unusual, especially when one considers the more numerous and significant differences the Greek recensions have with one another in other sections of IGT. This shared similarity with respect to the text of Jesus' alpha lesson, together with the unusual vocabulary it employs, might best be explained by Aasgaard's belief (noted below) that Jesus' exposition of the nature and meaning of the first letter functioned as a parody deployed in the form of a jingle, thus making it both memorable and resistant to significant alteration.

Interpreted this way, Jesus' exegesis emerges as a jingle consisting of a series of meaningful, half-sensical, and non-sensical words. It appears to be organized in patterns that make it easy to memorize: it has similar word beginnings (ὁμο-, ἰσο-), and endings (-μένους, -οντας), alliteration (β-/τ-/δ-, ε-/α-/ο-), and elements of rhyme (-πολεῖς, -γενεῖς) and rhythm. These features can very much account for the similarities among the variants, and also for the combination in Gs of fragments from Ga and Gd (see p. 21). The jingle is a form which easily allows for inclusion and exclusion of such elements.

In this interpretation, the passage can also be seen as a distortion and parody of reading exercises familiar to anyone having attended the antique school and—as a popular jingle—also to others. It would have been an easily memorable piece, well fit for being recited and performed, and with much playfulness in its formulations.

From this the function of the passage within 1 Teacher (6-8) becomes clearer. Within the narrative, Jesus' explanation of the alpha leaves the teacher and others overwhelmed as for his wisdom: they are unable to understand and explore the depths of his words. As a result, they are put to shame, as is shown in Zacchaeus' subsequent lament (7:1-4). For the real-life audience of IGT, however, the passage will have functioned differently. For most of them, it would be obvious that this was a parody, and that its series of words was only partly, or not at all, comprehensible—they could boast of having a knowledge that the poor teacher lacked. They would sense what Jesus was at and could amuse themselves with the shortcomings of such an authority figure. Here, a teacher falls pray [sic] to teachers' own strategies—one of their power tools, the neck-breaking word exercise, is now applied to one of their own kind, to his great detriment. And even for those in IGT's audience who might not perceive the raillery, the alpha exegesis would appear entertaining, serve as a curiosity-inspiring riddle, and encourage admiration of Jesus' learning."

Appendix 4:

Additional Episodes from Jesus' Childhood

In addition to the stories recounted in the Greek manuscripts of IGT, there are other episodes from Jesus' childhood which are found exclusively (with the exception of one Greek manuscript) in the versions of IGT translated into other languages. Below is a list of their contents and in which versional languages they appear.[30]

1. Jesus rides a sunbeam.
Found in the Latin Pseudo-Matthew, Armenian, Ethiopian, late-Medieval Syriac, Provençal, Old English, and Slavonic versions.

2. Jesus tears down and rebuilds a pagan temple.
Found in the Latin Pseudo-Matthew, the Arabic Infancy Gospel, and Slavonic versions.

3. Jesus heals a man's eye.
Found in four of the medieval Slavonic translations and distantly echoed in the Arabic Infancy Gospel.

4. Jesus turns children into swine.
Found in the Provençal, Old English, the Arabic Infancy Gospel, and Slavonic versions.

5. Jesus and the dyer.
Found in truncated form in one Greek manuscript (Paris, *A. F. Gr 239*), and in the Armenian, Coptic, Old English, Provençal, Arabic Infancy Gospel, and Slavonic (Ukranian) versions.

6. Jesus and the blacksmith.
Found in two Slavonic manuscripts.

---

[30] The list that follows is based on information assembled from Aasgaard, *The Childhood of Jesus*, 245-251 and Rosén, *The Slavonic Translation*, 44-45.

7. Jesus plays with lions.
Found in some of the Latin versions.

8. Jesus makes Joseph raise a dead man.
Found in some of the Latin versions.

9. Jesus shares a meal with his family.
Found in some of the Latin versions.

10. Jesus miraculously repairs a king's throne.
Found in some of the Arabic versions.

11. Jesus turns children into goats.
Found in one Syriac manuscript and some of the Arabic versions.

12. Children make Jesus king.
Found in one Syriac manuscript and some of the Arabic versions.

13. Jesus heals a man with serpent.
Found in one Syriac manuscript.

14. Jesus heals a boy on an ass.
Found in one Syriac manuscript.

15. Jesus makes dead fish come alive.
Found in one Syriac manuscript.

16. Jesus heals a child's snakebite.
Found in one Syriac manuscript and some of the Arabic versions.

Aasgaard also lists a story in which Jesus heals a snake-poisoned boy (not, apparently, the same as Jesus' healing of James' snakebite in IGT 16), but gives no manuscript/version in which it appears.

Appendix 5:

IGT 2 and the Qur'an

Outside of Christianity, IGT is famous for containing the earliest account of Jesus' miraculous creation of living birds from clay (ch. 2), a story that is referenced in a text from a different, albeit related, religious tradition, that of Islam. In fact, the story appears twice in the Qur'an (610-632 CE): once at Sura 3:49 and the second time at Sura 5:110.[31]

Sura 3:45-9 retells with modifications and additions the Christian annunciation story (Luke 1:26-38), in which Mary is told by the angel Gabriel (who has been sent by God) that she would conceive and become the mother of Jesus:

> (Remember) when the angels said: "O Maryam (Mary)! Verily, Allah gives you the glad tidings of a Word ["Be!" – and he was! i.e. 'Iesa (Jesus) the son of Maryam (Mary)] from Him, his name will be the Messiah 'Iesa (Jesus), the son of Maryam (Mary), held in honour in this world and in the Hereafter, and will be one of those who are near to Allah." (3:45)

> "He will speak to the people in the cradle and in manhood, and he will be one of the righteous." (3:46)

> She said: "O my Lord! How shall I have a son when no man has touched me." He said: "So (it will be) for Allah creates what He wills. When He has decreed something, He says to it only: "Be!" and it is. (3:47)

> And He (Allah) will teach him ['Iesa (Jesus)] the Book and Al-Hikmah (i.e. the Sunnah, the faultless speech of the Prophets, wisdom, etc.), (and) the Taurat (Torah) and the Injeel (Gospel). (3:48)

---

[31] The English translations of the Qur'an used below are by Muhammad Taqi Al-Din Al-Hilali and Muhammad Muhsin Khan, *The Noble Quran* (Dar-us-Salam, 1999).

And will make him ['Iesa (Jesus)] a Messenger to the Children of Israel (saying): "I have come to you with a sign from your Lord, that **I design for you out of clay, as it were, the figure of a bird,** and breathe into it, **and it becomes a bird** by Allah's Leave; and I heal him who was born blind, and the leper, and I bring the dead to life by Allah's Leave. And I inform you of what you eat, and what you store in your houses. Surely, therein is a sign for you, if you believe. (3:49)

In Sura 5:110 the story of Jesus' miraculous creation of the bird is repeated almost verbatim with Sura 3:49:

"(Remember) when Allah will say (on the Day of Resurrection). "O 'Iesa (Jesus), son of Maryam (Mary)! Remember My Favour to you and to your mother when I supported you with Ruh-ul-Qudus [Jibrael (Gabriel)] so that you spoke to the people in the cradle and in maturity; and when I taught you writing, Al-Hikmah (the power of understanding), the Taurat (Torah) and the Injeel (Gospel); **and when you made out of the clay, as it were, the figure of a bird**, by My Permission, and you breathed into it, **and it became a bird** by My Permission, and you healed those born blind, and the lepers by My Permission, and when you brought forth the dead by My Permission;..."

The story in the Qur'an is clearly not exactly the same as the one found in IGT. In the Qur'an there is only one bird, not twelve. In the Qur'an Jesus breathes into the bird to "animate" it (perhaps in imitation of God's action regarding the creation of Adam in Genesis 2:7); he does not clap his hands and cry out a command to them as in IGT. The single most important difference, of course, is that the Jesus of the Qur'an can only accomplish this and the other miraculous deeds listed in Sura 3:49 and Sura 5:110 because he has Allah's leave/permission, not because he is divine himself.

GLOSSARY

A α

ἄβλεπτος, -ον, *without sight, blind*

ἀγανακτέω, *be angry*

ἄγγελος, ὁ, *angel*; (CG) *messenger*

ἅγιος, -α, -ον, *holy*

ἀγνοέω (contracted form, ἀγνοῶ), *be ignorant, do not know*

ἄγω, ἄξω, ἤγαγον, (CG) *lead, take, bring*; (LG) *go*

ἀγών, -ῶνος, ὁ, *concern, trepidation; struggle, fight, contest*

ἀγωνίζομαι, *strive, do one's best*

ἀδελφός, ὁ, *brother*

ἀδικέω, *wrong, injure*

αἴρω, ἀρῶ, ἦρα, *take, take up* or *away, remove*

αἰσχύνη, ἡ, *shame, disgrace*

αἰών, -ῶνος, ὁ, *age, generation, epoch, era*

ἄκαρπος, -ον, *infertile, barren, unfruitful*

ἀκμάζω, *be at full bloom, be at one's prime* or *perfection, flourish*

ἀκολουθέω, *follow, accompany*

ἀκούω, *hear*

ἀκροάομαι, *listen to*

ἀκριβῶς, adv., *carefully, with care*

ἀλαλάζω, *clang, wail loudly*

ἀληθή, -ές, *true, truthful*

ἀληθῶς, *truly, in truth*

ἀλληγορία, ἡ, *allegory*

ἀλλός, -ή, -ό, *another, other*

ἄλφα, τό, (indecl.) *alpha*

ἀλφάβητον, τό, (LG) *alphabet*

ἄλων, -ος, ἡ, *threshing floor*

ἁλωνίζω, (LG) *thresh; work on a threshing-floor*

ἀμάχιμος, -ον, (unattested word) *not antagonistic* (?)

ἀμήν, (LG transliterated from Hebrew) *amen; so be it; truly, indeed.*

ἀναβλέπω, *look up*

ἀναγγέλλω, *bring back tidings of, report*

ἀναγι(γ)νώσκω, *read (aloud)*

ἀνακράζω, *cry out*

ἀναλογίος, ὁ, (Medieval Greek word not attested before the 10th century) *desk*

83

ἀνάπηρος, ὁ, *cripple*

ἀναχωρέω, *go back*

ἀνέρχομαι, ἀνελεύσομαι, ἀνεξῆλθον, *go up, go back*

ἄνθρωπός, ὁ, *man, human being*

ἀνίστημι, ἀναστήσω, ἀνέστησα, *make X stand up, raise X*; (LG) *raise* (from the dead); (2nd aor.) ἀνέστην, *stand up, rise*

Ἄννα, ὁ, (indecl.) *Annas*

ἀνόητος, -ον, *foolish*

ἀνοίγω (LG form of ἀνοίγνυμι; three aor. forms occur in LG: ἀνέῳξα, ἠνέῳξα, ἤνοιξα), *open*

ἀντλέω, *draw water*

ἀνυπότακτος, -ον, (LG) *unruly, insubordinate*

ἄνω, adv., *above*

ἄνωθεν, adv., *from above*

ἀξίνη, ἡ, *ax*

ἀξιόω, (contracted form, ἀξιῶ) (LG) *ask, request, beg*

ἀξίως, adv., *in a manner worthy of or suitable to*; *deservedly*

ἀπάγω, ἀπάξω, ἀπήγαγον, *lead away*

ἀπατάω, *deceive*

ἄπειρος, -ον, *inexperienced (in), unacquainted (with), ignorant (of)*

ἀπέρχομαι, ἀπελεύσομαι, ἀπῆλθον, *go, go away, depart*

ἀπλόω, *unfold, stretch out*

ἀπό, (prep. + gen.) *from, away from*; *by*

ἀποθνήσκω, ἀποθανοῦμαι, ἀπέθανον, *die*

ἀποκρίνομαι, *answer, reply*; (aor. pass. ἀπεκρίθην, ἀποκριθῆναι, and ἀποκριθείς, which first appear in LG, have the same meaning as the CG mid.)

ἀπολλύμι, ἀπολέσω / ἀπολῶ, ἀπώλεσα, *destroy, kill*; *lose*; (mid.) *die*; *be lost, perish*

ἀπολογία, ἡ, *defense*

ἀπολύω, *send away, let go, set free, release*

ἀποξηραίνω, *dry up, scorch*; (pass.) *be completely dried up*; *wither*; *become stiff*

ἀπορέω, *be at a loss, be perplexed*

ἀποστέλλω, *send*; *send out or away*

ἀποστοματίζω, (LG) *attack with questions, question sharply*; (CG) *dictate*; *recite, repeat by heart*

ἀποστρέφω, *turn one away, put to flight*; (mid./pass.) *turn back, return*

ἀποτυφλόω, (LG) *blind, make blind*; (pass.) *be or become blind*

ἄπτω, *light, ignite*; (mid. + gen.) *take hold of, touch*

ἀρετή, ἡ, *moral excellence, goodness, virtue*

ἀρκετός, -ή, -όν, (LG) *sufficient*

ἄροτρον, τό, *plow*
ἀρχή, ἡ, *beginning*
ἄρχω, *rule, govern*; (mid.) *begin*
ἀσεβής, -ές, *ungodly, godless, unholy*
αὐστηρός, -ά, -όν, *austere, harsh*
αὐτός, -ή, -ό, (CG, pron. in gen., dat., acc.) *him, her, it, them*; (LG, pron. in all cases) *he, she, it, they*

Β β

βάλλω, *throw, hit*; (mid.) *put about oneself, wear*
βάσις, -εως, ἡ, *foot* (of the body)
βαστάζω, *carry, carry off* or *away (a body for burial)*
βεβηλόω, (LG) *desecrate, violate*
βῆτα, τό, (indecl.) *beta*
βιάζομαι, (mid.) *exercise force, use force, force one's way*; (pass.) *suffer violence*
βιβλίον, τό, *roll, scroll, book*
βλέμμα, -ατος, *look, glance*
βλέπω, *see; look* (at or *on*); *be able to see, gain one's sight*
βουλεύω, *plan, decide; deliberate, consider*; (mid.) *determine, resolve*
βρέφος, -ους, τό, *baby, infant*

Γ γ

γάρ, *for, for you see.*
γαστήρ, -τρός, ἡ, *womb*
γειτονία, ἡ, *neighborhood*
γελάω, *laugh*
γεμίζω, *fill*
γεννάω, *be father of, give birth to*; (pass.) *be born*
γέρων, -οντος, ὁ, *old man, grown man*
γηγενής, -ές, *earthborn*
γί(γ)νομαι, *become*
γι(γ)νώσκω, *know, have knowledge of, understand*
γνήσιος, -α, -ον, *legitimate, real, true, loyal*
γνωρίζω, *make known*

γονεύς, γονέως, ὁ, *father*; (pl.) *parents*
γράμμα, -ατος, τό, *letter*; (pl.) *letters, writing*
γραμματεύς, -έως, ὁ, *scribe, expert in the Jewish law; clerk, scholar*
γράφω, *write*
γυνή, -αικός, ἡ, *woman, wife*

Δ δ

δάκνω, δήξομαι, ἔδακον, *bite*
δαμάζω, *subdue, tame; control*
δέ, *but, to the contrary, rather; and; now, then, so.*
δεῖ, (impersonal) *it is necessary, must; should, ought; it is proper*
δένδρον, τό, *tree*
δέω, *tie, bind*
δή, *indeed; then, therefore, now*
δῆγμα, -ατος, τό, *bite, sting*
διά, (prep. + gen.) *through*; (LG) *because of, on account of*; (prep. + acc.)
  because of, on account of
διάβασις, -εως, ἡ, *ford*
διαμένω, *stand firm, stand by*
διάνοια, ἡ, *mind, understanding*
διαρρήγνυμι, (LG) *bump (hard)*; (CG) *break through, split asunder*
διασχίζω, *split in two, cut through*
διδασκαλεῖον, τό, *school*
διδασκαλία, -ας, ἡ, *teaching, instruction*
διδάσκαλος, ὁ, *teacher*
διδάσκω, *teach*
δίδωμι, δώσω, ἔδωκα, *give*
διέρχομαι, διελεύσομαι, διῆλθον, *go or pass through*
διετηρέω, *keep, keep faithfully*
διηγέομαι, *describe in full; tell, relate*
διότι, *because*
δίστεγος, -ον, (LG) *of two stories, two-storied*
διστόμος, -ον, *two-sided, with two corners*
διώκω, (LG) *persecute; drive out or away*; (CG) *pursue, chase; prosecute*
δοκέω, *think, suppose, imagine*
δόξα, ἡ, *glory*
δύναμαι, (+ inf.) *be able, can*

δύναμις, -εως, ἡ, *power, supernatural power*
δύο, *two*
δώδεκα, *twelve*
δωδεκαετής, -ές, *twelve years old*

Ε ε

ἑβραϊκος, -ή, -όν, *Hebrew, Aramaic*
ἐγκαλέω, *accuse*
ἐγώ, ἐμοῦ / μου, ἐμοί / μοι, ἐμέ / με, *I, me.*
ἔθνος, ἔθνους, τό, (LG) *Gentile* (i.e., non-Jew); (CG) *tribe, people*
ἔθος, -ους, τό, *custom, habit*
εἰμί, ἔσομαι, ἦν, *be; exist*
εἰς, (prep. + acc.) *into, to*; (LG) *in, on, at, for*
εἷς, μία, ἔν, *one*
εἰσέρχομαι, εἰσελεύσομαι, εἰσῆλθον, *enter, go in*
εἶτα, adv., *then, next*
εἴτε...εἴτε, *either...or, whether...or*
ἐκ, ἐξ, (prep. + gen.) *from, out of*
ἑκατόν, *one hundred*
ἐκεῖ, adv., *there, that place*
ἐκεῖθεν, adv., *from there*
ἐκεῖνος, -ή, -ό, *that*; (pl.) *those*
ἐκκακέω, (LG) *be fainthearted, lack courage, despair; grow weary*
ἐκπλήσσομαι, (2nd aor.) ἐξεπλάγην, *be amazed*
ἐκτείνω, *stretch out, extend*
ἐκτρέφω, ἐκθρέψω, ἐξέθρεψα, *raise, rear (children)*
ἐκχέω, (ἐξεχέα, LG aor.) *pour out*
ἑλληνικός, -ή, -όν, *Greek*
ἐμβλέπω, *look straight at, look at*
ἐμός, -ή, -όν, *my, mine*
ἐν, (prep. + dat.) *in, by, by means of, among*; (LG) *into, on*
ἐναλλάκτος, ὁ, (unattested) *crossbeam* (?)
ἐνθυμέομαι (contracted form, ἐνθυμοῦμαι), *reflect on, ponder, think deeply of*
ἐνοικέω, *live in*
ἑξαετής, -ές, *six years old*
ἔξαιμος, -ον, (LG) *drained of blood*
ἐξέρχομαι, ἐξελεύσομαι, ἐξῆλθον, *go out, depart*

ἔξεστι(ν), (impersonal + inf.) *it is allowed* or *possible*

ἐξίστημι, (2ⁿᵈ aor.) ἐξέστη, (LG) *be amazed* or *astonished; be deranged*

ἔξω, adv., *out, outside;* (+ gen.) *outside, out of*

ἑορτή, ἡ, *festival, feast*

ἐπαίρω, ἐπαρῶ, ἐπῆρα, (LG) *take, take away;* (CG) *lift, raise (up)*

ἐπάνω, (+ gen.) *on, upon*

ἐπειδή, conj., *since, because, for; when, after*

ἔπειτα, adv., *then, afterwards, next*

ἐπερωτάω, *ask*

ἐπί, (prep. + dat.) *at; on; upon; because, for;* (prep. + acc.) *on, upon; for; to;* (LG) *at; in the face of*

ἐπιλαμβάνω, ἐπιλήψομαι, ἐπέλαβον, *take, seize;* (mid. + gen.) *take, take hold of, lay hold of*

ἐπιλύω, (LG) *explain; settle (a dispute);* (CG) *loose, untie, set free*

ἐπιστήμη, ἡ, *knowledge*

ἐπισπάω, *draw* or *drag after* one; (mid.) *take on*

ἐπιτάσσω, *order, command*

ἐπιτηδεύω, *practice;* (LG) *drill*

ἐργάζομαι, *do, accomplish; work*

ἔργον, τό, *work, deed*

ἔρχομαι, ἐλεύσομαι, ἦλθον, *come, go*

ἐρωτάω, *ask (a question)*

ἕτερος, -α, -ον, *other, another*

ἑτοιμασία, ἡ, (LG) *readiness; preparation*

ἕτοιμος, -η, -ον, *carried into effect, already done*

ἔτος, -ους, τό, *year*

εὐθέως, adv., *immediately, at once*

εὐθύς, adv., *immediately, at once; straight, directly;* (LG) *then*

εὐλογέω, (LG) *bless;* (CG) *speak well of, praise, honor*

εὑρίσκω, εὑρήσω, ηὗρον / εὗρον, *find*

ἐφίστημι, ἐπιστήσω, ἐπέστησα, *consider, fix one's mind on, give one's attention to*

ἔχιδνα, -ης, ἡ, *snake, viper*

ἔχω, ἕξω, ἔσχον, *have; hold;* (+ inf.) *can, be able, must; have* (sc. the power)

ἕως, conj., *until, as far as;* (LG, prep. + gen.) *to, until, as far as, throughout, to the point of, for*

Z ζ

Ζακχαῖος, ὁ, *Zacchaeus*

ζάω, (unattested hypothetical form) *live, be alive*

Ζῆνον, ὁ, *Zeno* (a common name in the ancient world; the most famous Zeno being the founder of the Stoic school of philosophy, Zeno of Citium).

ζητέω, *seek, look for*

ζυγός, ὁ, *yoke*

ζυγόστομος, -ον, (unattested word) *crossbars* (?)

ζωή, ἡ, *life*

H η

ἤ, conj., *or*

ἡδέως, adv., *gladly*

ἡλικία, ἡ, *age*

ἡμεῖς, ἡμῶν, ἡμῖν, ἡμᾶς, (pl.) *we, us.*

ἡμέρα, ἡ, *day*

Θ ϑ

ϑαμβέω, *be astounded, amazed*

ϑάνατος, ὁ, *death*

ϑανατόω, *die*

ϑαρρέω, *be full of courage, act boldly, be confident*

ϑαῦμα, -ατος, τό, (LG) *miracle*; (CG) *wonder, marvel*

ϑαυμάζω, *be amazed, wonder at; admire*

ϑέλω, (+ inf.) *wish, desire, want*

ϑεός, ὁ, *God, god*

ϑερίζω, *reap, harvest, gather*

ϑηρίον, τό, (LG) *poisonous animal, reptile, snake*; (CG) *wild animal, beast*

ϑόρυμος, ὁ, *confusion, disturbance*

ϑρασύς, -εῖα, -ύ, *bold, spirited, courageous*

ϑρηνέω, *lament, sing a funeral song*

ϑυμόομαι, *be furious*

ϑύρα, ἡ, *door*

Θωμᾶς, ὁ, *Thomas*

I ι

'Ιάκωβος, ὁ, *James; Jacob*
ἰάομαι, *heal, cure; restore*
ἴδιος, -α, -ον, *private*
ἰδού, adv., *look!*
ἱερόν, τό, *temple, temple precinct*
'Ιερουσαλήμ, ἡ, (indecl.) *Jerusalem*
'Ιησοῦς, 'Ιησοῦ, Ιησοῦ, Ιησοῦν, ὁ, *Jesus*
ἵνα, conj. + subju., *in order that* (expressing purpose), *so that* (expressing result)
'Ιουδαῖος, ὁ, *Judean, Jew*
ἰσόμετρος, -ον, (LG) *of equal measure*
ἰσοποιέω, (unattested) *make equal*
ἴσος, -η, -ον, *equal, the same*
'Ισραηλίτης, -ου, ὁ, *Israelite*
ἵστημι, στήσω, ἔστησα, *make X stand; stop X; set X (up);* (2nd aor.)
    ἔστην, (perf.) ἔστηκα, *stand*
ἰσχύω, (LG) *be able, can;* (CG) *be strong, mighty,* or *powerful; prevail*
ἴσως, adv., *perhaps*
ἰτέα, -ας, ἡ, *willow*
'Ιωσήφ, ὁ, (indecl.), *Joseph*

K κ

καθαρός, -ά, -όν, *clean, pure*
καθέζομαι, *sit, sit down*
καθηγητής, -οῦ, ὁ, (LG) *teacher*
καθίστημι, (2nd aor.) κατέστην *stand, stand quiet*
καθώς, adv., *as, just as*
καί, (conj.) *and, also, but, even*
καιρός, ὁ, *time, appointed* or *proper time, season*
κακός, -ή, -όν, *bad, evil*
καλέω, *summon, call in*
καλός, -ή, -όν, (LG) *good; beautiful, fine*
καλῶς, adv., *well; rightly, correctly*
κανών, -όνος, ὁ, *straight bar* or *line*
καρδία, ἡ, *heart; mind*
καρπός, ὁ, *fruit*

καρποφορέω, *bear fruit, be productive*

κατά, (prep. + acc.) *with respect* or *reference to, according to*

καταβάλλω, *throw down*

καταλείπω, *leave, leave behind*; (pass. often =) *remain*

καταμέμφομαι, *find great fault with, blame greatly, accuse*

καταπαύω, *stop, cease, end*

καταπηδάω, *leap down*

κατάρα, ἡ, *curse*

καταράομαι, *call down curses upon, curse*

κατατείνω, *stretch, stretch out*; (pass.) *stretch on the ground; lay at full length*

καταφιλέω, *kiss*

καταφυσάω, (LG) *blow on*

κατεργάζομαι, *do, accomplish*

κάτω, adv., *down; below, beneath*

κεῖμαι, κείσομαι, *lie*

κεφάλαιον, τό, *main point*

κεφαλή, ἡ, *head*

κλάδος, ὁ, *small branch*

κλαίω, *cry, weep, weep for*

κλάω, *break*

κοιλία, ἡ, *womb; stomach, belly*

κολακεία, ἡ, *flattery*

κόλασις, -εως, ἡ, *punishment*

κολοβός, -όν, *short*

κόρος, ὁ, *cor* (a dry measure of around 10-12 bushels)

κοσμοποιία, ἡ, *creation of the world*

κόσμος, ὁ, *world, universe*

κράββατος, ὁ, (LG; a [Macedonian?] loan word) *bed, cot*

κράζω, *cry out, shriek*

κρατέω, (LG) *take hold of*

κρίσις, -εως, ἡ, *condemnation, punishment*

κρούω, *strike, hit*

κτίζω, *create, make*

κύμβαλον, τό, *cymbal*

κύριος, ὁ, (LG) *Lord* (title of God in the Old Testament and of Jesus Christ in the New Testament); (CG) *lord, master, head* (of a family/household); *sir*

κώμη, ἡ, *village*

κωφός, -ή, -όν, *deaf; dumb, mute*

Λ λ

λάκκος, ὁ, *pond*

λαλέω, (LG) *say, speak, tell*; (CG) *talk (aimlessly), chat, babble*

λαμβάνω, λήψομαι, ἔλαβον, *take*

λαός, ὁ, *people*

λέγω, ἐρῶ, εἶπον, *say, speak, tell*

λιποθυμέω, *lose consciousness, pass out*

λογίζομαι, *think, suppose*

λόγος, ὁ, *word, speech*

λοιπόν, adv., *from now on, henceforth*; *in addition*

λυπέω, *vex, cause grief* or *pain to X, injure*; (pass.) *be sad, sorrowful* or
  distressed; *grieve*

λύω, *release*

Μ μ

μαθητής, οῦ, ὁ, *student*

μακάριος, -α, -ον, *blessed, fortunate, happy*

μάλιστα, adv., *most, most of all, very much, especially, too much*

μᾶλλον, adv., *more, much more*; *rather, instead*

μανθάνω, *learn, understand*

Μαρία, ἡ, *Mary*

μαρτυρέω, *bear witness, give evidence, testify*; *attest, affirm, speak well of*

μασθός, ὁ, (LG alternative form of μαστός) *breast*

μεγαλεῖος, -α, -ον, *magnificent, splendid, mighty*

μέγας, μεγάλη, μέγα, *large, great*

μένω, *remain, stay*; (LG) *live*; *continue*

μέσος, -η, -ον, *middle, in the middle*; (μέσον, adv.) *in the middle*

μεστός, -ή, -όν, *full*

μέτα, (prep. + gen.) *with*; (prep. + acc.) *after*

μήτηρ, μητρός, ἡ, *mother*

μικροθαύμαστος, -ον, (unattested word) *marveling at trifles*; *easily impressed*

μικρός, -ά, -ό, *little, small*

μιμνήσκω, *remind*; (mid./pass.) *remember*

μισέω, *hate*

μνημονεύω, *remember, keep in mind*; *make mention of*

μονός, -ή, -όν, *alone, only, single*

μυστήριον, τό, *secret, mystery*

N ν

νεανίσκος, ὁ, *young man*

νεκρός, ὁ, *corpse, dead body*

νεκρός, -ά, -όν, *dead, lifeless*

νεότης, νεότητος, ἡ, (LG) *youth;* (CG) *youthful spirit, impetuosity, rashness*

νεώτερος, -α, -ον, (LG) *young, younger, youngest*

νήπιος, -α, -ον, *baby, infant, child;* (CG often =) *childish, silly*

νικάω, *conquer, overcome, defeat*

νοέω, *think over, consider; understand*

νομίζω, *think, suppose, assume*

νόμος, ὁ, (LG) *law* (i.e., the Jewish sacred tradition, as found, e.g., in the Old Testament); (CG) *custom, usage, law; pasture; province, district*

νοσέω, *be sick*

νουθετέω, *admonish, reprimand*

νοῦς, νοῦ, ὁ, *mind*

νῦν, adv., *now*

Ξ ξ

ξένος, -η, -ον, *strange, foreign, unusual*

ξηραίνω, *dry up;* (pass.) *become dry; wither; become stiff*

ξύλον, τό, *wood; piece of wood*

O o

ὁδεύω, *go, travel, journey*

ὁδός, ὁδοῦ, ἡ, *road, way, journey*

ὀδυνάομαι, *be in great pain; be deeply distressed* or *worried*

οἶδα, (perf. with pres. meaning) *know*

οἰκέω, *live, dwell*

οἰκοδομή, ἡ, (LG) *building, structure, house*

οἶκος, ὁ, *house, home, dwelling*

οἴμοι, *ah me! poor me!*

ὀκτώ, *eight*

ὀλίγος, -η, -ον, *little, small;* (pl.) *few*

ὅλος, -η, -ον, *whole, entire*

ὁμογενής, -ές, *of the same race, family,* or *type*

ὅμως, conj., *nevertheless*

ὄνομα, -ατος, τό, *name*

ὄντως, adv., *really, certainly, indeed;* (used as attributive adj.) *real*

ὀξυσμένος, -ον, (unattested word) *of sharp strength* (?)

ὀξύτης, -τος, ἡ, *quickness*

ὅπως, *that, in order that*

ὁράω, ὄψομαι, εἶδον, *see*

ὀργίζω, *make X angry;* (pass.) *grow angry, be angry* or *furious*

ὀργή, ἡ, *anger, wrath*

ὀρθῶς, adv., *rightfully, correctly, properly*

ὅς, ἥ, ὅ, rel. pron., *who, whose, whom, which, that*

ὅσος, -η, -ον, *as great as, as much as;* (pl.) *as many as*

ὅσπερ, ἥπερ, ὅπερ, rel. pron., emphatic forms, *who, whose, whom, which, that*

ὅταν (ὅτε + ἄν; + subju.), *when, whenever*

ὅτε, conj., *when*

ὅτι, conj., *that, because*

οὐδείς, οὐδεμία, οὐδέν, *no one, nothing; no*

οὐδέποτε, adv., *never*

οὖν, adv., *therefore, then*

οὔπω, adv., *not yet*

οὐράνιος, -ον, *heavenly, from heaven*

οὔτε, conj., *and not, not, nor*

οὔτε...οὔτε, conj., *neither...nor*

οὗτος, αὕτη, τοῦτο, *this;* (pl.) *these*

οὕτως, adv., *so, thus; as follows*

οὐχί, (emphatic form of οὐ) *not; no, no indeed*

ὅτε, adv., *when*

ὄχλος, ὁ, *crowd, multitude*

ὄψις, -εως, ἡ, *face*

Π π

παιδευτήριον, τό, *school*

παιδεύω, *instruct, teach*

παιδικός, -ή, -όν, *child-like, playful, pertaining to one's childhood;* in CG τὰ
παιδικά is a term of romantic affection meaning *darling* or *favorite*

παιδίον, τό, (diminutive of παῖς, ὁ or ἡ) *little* or *young child, child*

παίζω, *play*

παῖς, παίδος, ὁ or ἡ, *boy, girl, son, daughter, child*

πάλιν, adv., *again, once more, in turn*

παλίον, τό, (LG, loan word from Latin; more often spelled πάλλιον) *cloak*

πάνυ, adv., *altogether, very, exceedingly*

παρά, (prep. + gen.) *from, by*

παραβολή, ἡ, (LG) *parable, proverb*; (CG) *comparison, illustration, analogy*

παραγγέλλω, παραγγελῶ, παρήγγειλα, *order, command*

παραδίδωμι, παραδώσω, παρέδωκα, *hand over, give*

παράδοξος, -ον, *incredible, unusual*

παράκλησις, -εως, ἡ, (LG) *consolation*; (CG) *address, exhortation*

παραδίδωμι, παραδώσω, παρέδωκα, *hand* or *give over; entrust, commit, give*

παραινέω, *advise*

παρακαλέω (contracted form, παρακαλῶ), *beg*

παραλάμβανω, παραλήψομαι, παρέλαβον, *take, receive, accept, take charge of*

παραυτά, adv., *at once, immediately*

παραχρῆμα, adv., *on the spot, at once*

πάρειμι, (πάρα + εἰμί) *be present* or *here; be present so as to help; have come*

πάρειμι, (πάρα + εἶμι) *go by, go pass, pass by*

παρέχω, παρασχήσω, παρέσχον, *produce, bring about, provide*

παρηγορέω, *comfort, console*

παρίστημι, παραστήσω, (1ˢᵗ aor.) παρέστησα, *present, show*; (2ⁿᵈ aor.) παρέστην, (perf.) παρέστηκα, *stand by, be present*

παροργίζω, *make angry*

πάροχος, ὁ, (LG) *passenger*

πᾶς, πᾶσα, πᾶν, *all, every, whole*

πάσχα, τό, (indecl.) *Passover*

πάσχω, πείσομαι, ἔπαθον, *suffer*

πατήρ, πατρός, ὁ, *father*

παύω, *stop*; (mid.) *cease from*

πεῖρα ἡ, *experience*

πέμπω, *send*

πένθος, -ους, τό, *(public) mourning, sorrow, grief*

πενταετής, -ές, *five years old*

πέντε, *five*

περί, (prep. + gen.) *about, concerning*

περιίστημι, περιστήσω, περιέστησα, (LG) *stand around*

περιλαμβάνω, *embrace*

πέτομαι, *fly*

πηλός, ὁ, *clay, earth, mud*

πικραίνω, *make sharp or bitter to the taste*; (pass.) *feel exasperated, bitter*, or *angry*

πίπτω, πεσοῦμαι, ἔπεσον, *fall*

πιστεύω, *believe*

πλάσσω, *form, mold, shape*

πλειστάκις, adv., *many times*

πληγόω (LG alternative form of πλήσσω), *strike*

πλήν, (+ gen.) *except, except for, besides, but*

πλήσσω, *strike*

πλουσίος, -α, -ον, *rich*

πνεῦμα, -ατος, τό, (LG) *Spirit* (of God); (CG) *wind, breeze, breath, spirit*

πόθεν, adv., *from where*

ποιέω, *make, produce, create*; *do*

ποῖος, -α, -ον, *what, which*; *what kind of*

πολύς, πολλή, πολύ, *much*; (pl.) *many*

πόνος, ὁ, *pain, suffering*

πορεύομαι, *go, walk, journey*

πόσος, -η, -ον, *how much, how many*

πότε, adv., *when*

ποτέ, (enclitic particle) *ever*

πουλίον, τό, (LG, sometimes spelled πουλλίον) *bird*

πούς, πόδος, ὁ, *foot* (LG often adds -ν to the 3rd declension acc. sing. ending)

πρᾶγμα, -τος, τό, *matter, thing, affair*

πράττω, *do, act*

πρεσβύτερος, ὁ, *elder* (here of the Jewish religious leaders)

πρό, (prep. + gen.) *before*

προθυμία, ἡ, *willingness, readiness, eagerness, zeal*

πρός, (prep. + acc.) *to*

προσγελάω, *look laughing at, smile upon*

προσεγγίζω, *approach*

προσέρχομαι, προσελεύσομαι, προσῆλθον, (+ dat.) *approach*; *go or come forward, approach*

προσέχω, προσέξω, προσέσχον, *pay close attention to*

προσκαλέω, *call to, call on*; (mid.) *call to oneself, summon*

προκόπτω, *advance, progress, grow*

προσκυνέω, *worship, fall down and worship*

προστάσσω, *command, order*

πρόσωπον, τό, *face*

προφήτης, ου, ὁ, *prophet*; (LG) οἱ προφῆται = *prophetic books of the Hebrew Scriptures/Old Testament*

πρῶτοι, οἱ, *the leaders*

πρῶτον, adv., *first, first of all*

πρῶτος, -η, -ον, *first*

πτῶμα, -ατος, τό, *body, corpse*

πτωχός, -ή, -όν, *poor*

πῦρ, -ος, τό, *fire*

πῶς, adv., *how?, in what manner* or *way?*

Ρ ρ

ῥέω, *flow, run*

ῥήγνυμι (also ῥηγνύω and ῥήσσω), *break, break in pieces*; (pass.) *burst (apart)*

ῥῆμα, ῥήματος, τό, *word*

ῥίζα, ἡ, *root*

ῥυάκιον, τό, (diminutive of ῥύαξ, -ακος, ὁ) *(small) rushing stream*

ῥύαξ, -ακος, ὁ, *rushing stream*

ῥύομαι, *save, rescue, deliver*

Σ σ

σάββατον, τό, *Sabbath*

σιγάω, *be silent*

σιωπάω, *be silent*

σημεῖον, τό, (LG) *miraculous sign, miracle*; (CG) *sign*

σῖτος, ὁ, *grain, wheat*

σκιρτάω, *spring, leap*

Σοδομίτης, -ου, ὁ, *Sodomite.*

σός, -ή, -όν, *your*

σοφία, ἡ, *wisdom, insight, intelligence, knowledge*

σοφῶς, adv., *wisely*

σπείρω, *sow*

σπόρος, ὁ, *sowing*

σπουδαίως, adv., *with haste, energetically*

σταυρός, ὁ, *cross*

στέγη, ἡ, *roof*

στῆθος, -ους, τό, *chest, breast*

στοιχεῖον, τό, *letter, element*

στόμα, -ατος, τό, *mouth*

στρουθίον, τό, (LG diminutive of στρουθός, ὁ or ἡ) *sparrow*

σύ, σοῦ / σου, σοί / σοι, σέ / σε, (sing.) *you*

συγγενής, -οῦς, ὁ, *relative*

σύν, (prep. + dat.) *with*

συγκροτέω, *strike together*; (with χεῖρας) *clap one's hands (in joy)*

συγκρούω, *strike* or *crash together, collide* or *come into collision with*

συλλέγω, *collect, gather*

συνάγω, συνάξω, συνήγαγον, *bring* or *gather together*

συνδρομή, ἡ, *rushing together*

συνέρχομαι, συνελεύσομαι, συνῆλθον, *come together, gather*

σύνεσις, -εως, ἡ, *understanding, insight, intelligence*

συνίημι, συνήσω, συνῆκα, *understand, comprehend*

συνοδία, ἡ, *group of travelers*

σφόδρα, adv., *very, very much, greatly; strongly, violently*

σχίζω, *split, cut, chop*

σῴζω, *save, rescue, deliver; cure, make well*

T τ

τάλας, τάλαινα, τάλαν, *suffering, wretched*

τάξις, -εως, ἡ, *arrangement, order*

ταραχοποιός, -όν, (LG) *troublemaking*; ταραχοποιός, ὁ, *troublemaker*

τάχα, adv., *perhaps*

τείνω, *stretch, pull*

τέκνον, τό, *child*; (in the voc. for familiar address) *my child.*

τέκτων, -όνος, ὁ, *carpenter, builder*

τέλειος, -α, -ον, *complete, perfect*

τέλος, -ους, τό, *end*

τίθημι, θήσω, ἔθηκα, *put, place, lay, set*

τίς, τί, (gen. τίνος) interrog. pron. and adj., *who? which? what?*

τις, τι, (gen. τινος) indefinite pron., *someone; something; anyone; anything*

τοιγαροῦν, *therefore, then, for that very reason then*

τοιοῦτος, τοιαύτη, τοιοῦτο, *such*

τολμάω, *dare, be brave* or *bold enough*

τόπος, ὁ, place

τοσοῦτος, -αύτη, -οῦτον, so much, so great; (pl.) so many

τότε, adv., then, at that time

τρανής, -ές, piercing, clear, distinct

τρέχω, δραμοῦμαι, ἔδραμον, run

τρισάθλιος, -α, -ον, literally, thrice-miserable, triply-wretched, i.e., very miserable or wretched

τριστόμος, -ον, three-sided, with three corners

τρίτος, -η, -ον, third

τρυφερός, -ά, -όν, soft; in CL the adj. normally means delicate, dainty

τυγχάνω, happen (+ supplementary participle)

Υ υ

ὑγιής, -ές, sound, healthy; well, cured

ὑδρία, ἡ, water jug

ὕδωρ, ὕδατος, τό, water

υἱός, ὁ, son

ὑμεῖς, ὑμῶν, ὑμῖν, ὑμᾶς, (pl.) you.

ὑπάγω, ὑπάξω, ὑπήγαγον, (LG) go, go away, depart

ὑπάρχω (= εἰμί), be

ὑπό, (prep. + gen.) by; (prep. + acc.) under

ὑποκριτής, οῦ, ὁ, hypocrite, imposter

ὑποστρέφω, return, turn back

ὑποτάσσω, rule, control, subordinate; (pass.) be obedient to, obey

ὕψος, -ους, τό, height

ὑψόω, raise up, elevate; exalt

Φ φ

Φαρισαῖος, ὁ, Pharisee

φέρω, οἴσω, ἤνεγκα (CG more often ἤνεγκον), carry, bring, bear

φεύγω, flee, run away

φθέγγομαι, speak, utter

φίλος, ὁ, friend

φοβέομαι, be frightened or afraid (of), fear

φόβος, ὁ, fear

φρόνιμος, -ον, *wise, sensible, prudent, thoughtful, intelligent*
φρόνημα, -ατος, τό, *way of thinking, mind*
φρύγανον, τό, *dry wood, stick*
φύλλον, τό, *leaf*
φύσις, -εως, ἡ, *nature, being, essence*
φωνή, ἡ, *sound, noise, voice*

Χ χ

χαλκοῦς, -ῆ, -οῦν, *made of copper, brass*, or *bronze*
χαμαί, adv., *on* or *to the ground*
χαρακτήρ, -ῆρος, ὁ, *mark, point; distinctive mark, characteristic*
χαρίζομαι, *give generously* or *freely*
χάρις, -ιτος, ἡ, *grace, kindness, goodwill;* (LG) *a special manifestation of the divine presence, power,* or *glory*
χείρ, χειρός, ἡ, *hand*
χορεύω, *dance*
χοῦς, ὁ, *pitcher* (holding nearly 3 quarts)
Χριστός, ὁ, *the Anointed One/Messiah;* later a proper name (i.e., *Christ*)
χρόνος, ὁ, *time*
χώρα, ἡ, *land*

Ψ ψ

ψυχή, ἡ, *life, life-force, soul, spirit; mind, understanding; person, human being*

Ω ω

ὧδε, adv., *in this way, so, thus*
ὦμος, ὁ, *shoulder*
ὥρα, ἡ, *time*
ὡραιότης, -ητος, ἡ, (LG) *beauty; maturity*
ὠτίον, τό, (LG diminutive of οὖς, τό) *ear*

Notes

Notes

Notes

Notes

Made in United States
Cleveland, OH
21 March 2025

15347875R00072